How to use

In this issue

The 92 daily readings in this issue of *Explore* are designed to help you understand and apply the Bible as you read it each day.

It's serious!

We suggest that you allow 15 minutes each day to work through the Bible passage with the notes. It should be a meal, not a snack! Readings from other parts of the Bible can throw valuable light on the study passage. These cross-references can be skipped if you are already feeling full up, but they will expand your grasp of the Bible. *Explore* uses the NIV2011 Bible translation, but you can also use it with the NIV1984 or ESV translations.

Sometimes a prayer box will encourage you to stop and pray through the lessons—but it is always important to allow time to pray for God's Spirit to bring his word to life, and to shape the way we think and live through it.

We're serious!

All of us who work on Explore share a passion for getting the Bible into people's lives. We fiercely hold to the Bible as God's word— to honour and follow, not to explain away.

1 Find a time you can read the Bible each day

2 Find a place where you can be quiet and think

3 Ask God to help you understand

4 Carefully read through the Bible passage for today

5 Study the verses with Explore, taking time to think

6 Pray about what you have read

thegoodbook
COMPANY

BIBLICAL | RELEVANT | ACCESSIBLE

Welcome to Explore

Being a Christian isn't a skill you learn, like carpentry or flower arranging. Nor is it a lifestyle choice, like the kind of clothes you wear, or the people you choose to hang out with. It's about having a real relationship with the living God through his Son, Jesus Christ. The Bible tells us that this relationship is like a marriage.

It's important to start with this, because many Christians view the practice of daily Bible-reading as a Christian duty, or a hard discipline that is just one more thing to get done in our busy modern lives.

But the Bible is God speaking to us: opening his mind to us on how he thinks, what he wants for us and what his plans are for the world. And most importantly, it tells us what he has done for us in sending his Son, Jesus Christ, into the world. It's the way the Spirit shows Jesus to us, and changes us as we behold his glory.

The Bible is not a manual. It's a love letter. And as with any love letter, we'll want to treasure it, and make time to read and re-read it, so we know we are loved, and discover how we can please the One who loves us. Here are a few suggestions for making your daily time with God more of a joy than a burden:

- *Time:* Find a time when you will not be disturbed, and when the cobwebs are cleared from your mind. Many people have found that the morning is the best time as it sets you up for the day. If you're not a "morning person", then last thing at night or a mid-morning break might suit you. Whatever works for you is right for you.

- *Place:* Jesus says that we are not to make a great show of our religion *(see Matthew 6:5-6)*, but rather, to pray with the door to our room shut. Some people plan to get to work a few minutes earlier and get their Bible out in an office or some other quiet corner.

- *Prayer:* Although *Explore* helps with specific prayer ideas from the passage, try to develop your own lists to pray through. Use the flap inside the back cover to help with this. And allow what you read in the Scriptures to shape what you pray for yourself, the world and others.

- *Share:* As the saying goes: *expression deepens impression.* So try to cultivate the habit of sharing with others what you have learned. Why not join our Facebook group to share your encouragements, questions and prayer requests? Search for *Explore: For your daily walk with God.*

And remember, *it's quality, not quantity, that counts:* better to think briefly about a single verse than to skim through pages without absorbing anything, because it's about developing your relationship with the living God. The sign that your daily time with God is real is when you start to love him more and serve him more wholeheartedly.

Tim Thornborough and Carl Laferton
Editors

GENESIS: Previously…

Jacob the deceiver has tasted his own medicine as he has endured 20 years of deception and exploitation by his scheming uncle Laban. At last he's escaped…

Now he's headed for the promised land. But his two wives, 11 children and huge herds are not all he has with him…

Hedging your bets
Read Genesis 31:22-35

❓ *What does Rachel steal from her father?*

She is hedging her bets. She has not yet learned to trust wholeheartedly in the God of the Bible, and so she takes these "gods" to gain their blessing. (What is it with this family and stealing blessings?!)

❓ *How much blessing does she get from these gods?*

False gods never deliver. The other things we cling to in the hope they will give meaning and blessing to our lives always end up bringing difficulty and disappointment.

Showdown
Read Genesis 31:36-42

❓ *How has Jacob been treated by Laban?*
❓ *Why do you think he keeps stressing the number of years?*
❓ *So how was it that he was able to prosper in spite of Laban's scheming and mistreatment?*
❓ *How else do we see the true God protect Jacob and his family in this passage (see v 24, 29 and 35)?*

Why seek the blessing of pathetic carved "godlets" when the true God is with you?

In a few hundred years the children of Israel will be mistreated and exploited by a tyrannical ruler in Egypt. But again, God will see their hardship and rescue them.

Read Exodus 1:6-14, 3:1-10

The Bible is full of patterns and shadows to help us see how consistent and reliable God's character is!

Moans and stones
Read Genesis 31:43-55

Laban is petty and pathetic. He happily gave his daughters to Jacob, and he set Jacob's wages (and then repeatedly changed them). But we all have a tendency to justify ourselves and fail to see our own wrongdoing.

Jacob and his family faced serious danger at the beginning of the passage.

❓ *By the end, what guarantee of safety do they have from Laban?*
❓ *What title does Jacob give to God as he takes his oath in verse 53?*

In a world of scheming cheats and enslaving abusers, it is a great comfort to be able to cry out to a God who is worth fearing!

⌃ Pray

Pray that you would not be tempted to trust in other things for security and blessing but would look to God alone.

Out of the frying pan…

… and into the fire! Jacob has escaped from deceitful uncle Laban. But he is walking straight into the path of vengeful brother Esau. The life of faith is not one of ease.

God with us

Read Genesis 32:1-9

God promised to be with Jacob when he left the promised land in 28:15. Now he reminds him that he is still with him. David may have had this episode in mind when he wrote Psalm 34:7: "The angel of the LORD encamps around those who fear him, and he delivers them".

❷ *How is this confidence in God's protection immediately put to the test in Genesis 32:3-6?*
❷ *How does Jacob feel, and what does he do in response to this (v 7-9)?*

Just as important as what he does do is what he does not do. He may feel afraid and take precautions, but he does not disobey God by turning back.

Note too how he addresses Esau. Many years earlier he had deceived his brother so that he could take the blessing that was rightfully Esau's as firstborn.

❷ *But how does he address his brother here?*

Prayer…

Read Genesis 32:9-12

We have seen Jacob say and do many things over the last seven chapters—but this is the first time we have seen him pray.

❷ *What gives Jacob confidence as he prays to God for his protection?*

We can likewise pray with confidence when we are obeying God, when we recognise how much God has already blessed us in spite of our unworthiness, and when we trust in his promises.

… and planning

Reliance on God in prayer does not mean inaction. On the contrary, it makes action worthwhile.

Read Genesis 32:13-21

❷ *What does Jacob hope his gifts will achieve?*

⌃ Pray

Read Philippians 4:6-7

❷ *What things are causing you anxiety or stress as you face this day?*
❷ *Will you obey Paul's words here, following the example of Jacob as he prepared to meet his brother?*

Pray now!

Limping to victory

Jacob is full of fear and anxiety. So what does God do? Speak words of comfort? Send an army of angels? No—he attacks him in the dark and cripples him!

And it's the best thing that could have happened to Jacob...

Grappling with the grasper
Read Genesis 32:22-26

Jacob's family cross the river at night.

- ❷ *What happens when he is left alone in the darkness?*
- ❷ *Who is this mysterious man, according to verses 28-30?*
- ❷ *How does the wrestling match go to start with?*

Ever since he was a baby, Jacob has been a wrestler. His name means "grasper" or "deceiver". He has wrestled with his brother, with his father and with Laban (see Hosea 12:3-4). Each time he has come out on top. It looks as if this is going the same way—until God uses his supernatural power.

- ❷ *What does Jacob then do?*
- ❷ *Why do you think God does this to Jacob?*

God has humbled Jacob until all he can do is cling to God. His only hope is in God's blessing, and he clings to him for all he is worth.

Who are you?
Read Genesis 32:27-32

Why would the God who knows everything ask Jacob his name? Because Jacob's answer is also a confession. He is saying, "I am Grasper; I am Deceiver". God has brought him to the end of himself. His strength is broken, and he recognises his sinfulness. But God doesn't break him to destroy him. He has done it to prepare Jacob for blessing. He is now ready to cross into the promised land and to lead God's people. "Whoever conceals their sins does not prosper, but the one who confesses and renounces them finds mercy" (Proverbs 28:13).

⌄ Apply

We can only ever limp to glory. We will never be spiritually useful until we have been humbled by God. We never seem to be able to rely wholly on Jesus until we have come to the end of our own strength. Sometimes that's physical as with Jacob. But it might be financial, moral or emotional. As God says to Paul in 2 Corinthians 12:9, in our greatest weakness you and I discover that "[God's] grace is sufficient for you, for [God's] power is made perfect in weakness."

- ❷ *Where are you tempted to trust your own strength?*
- ❷ *How has God caused you to limp, but also to know his blessing?*

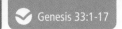
Brothers not-quite-united

Jacob and Esau enjoy a beautiful reunion. The bitter rivalry that tore their family apart is laid to rest. But it is clear that their lives are heading in different directions.

No small change

Read Genesis 33:1-11

The question we're left with at the end of chapter 32 is whether Jacob has really changed. He spent the first part of his life grasping and deceiving to get all he could. This included the blessing of the firstborn, which meant he would be "lord over [his] brothers" and that they would "bow down to [him]" (27:29).

❷ *What indications are there in 33:1-11 of a genuine repentance?*

It can be easy to say, "I'm sorry". True repentance involves real change, and this means making things right where possible.

❷ *How do we see this with Jacob?*

Jacob humbly bows to Esau, greets him as lord and generously gives him costly gifts—the very things he deceived Esau to get, he now gives back.

❷ *How does Esau respond?*

No small difference

The brothers have come back together, but there is a difference between them that means they will never really walk together. The narrator shows this subtly in v 4-11.

❷ *What does Jacob mention repeatedly as he explains how he's become so wealthy? What word does Esau never use?*

In the same way, God has been absent from Esau's life throughout these chapters. Esau has never cared about God or his own role as part of the covenant family. That's a big deal—it's not like ignoring his family's quirky Christmas traditions. He's ignoring their role in bringing salvation to a world condemned in sin.

Parting of the ways

Read Genesis 33:12-17

It's hard to know what to make of these verses. What is undeniable is that Jacob is right to head back to the promised land, in obedience to God's command (32:9), rather than head off with Esau. It's unclear though whether he's right to deceive his brother, or whether this is a culturally appropriate way to part ways.

☑ Apply

Real repentance—true change—often involves giving up what is precious to us.

❷ *Where have you seen this in your life?*
❷ *Where might you need to act on this right now?*

☒ Pray

Pray that the cost of true repentance would not keep you from truly turning to Jesus in trusting obedience.

Surprising reversals

Jacob has had a decisive, life-changing encounter with God. But habits, character and relationships don't change overnight. What happens next is truly upsetting.

....

Read Genesis 33:18 – 34:31

> ❓ *Read the whole passage. Who is never mentioned?*

None of the characters involved consider how to obey their God in the way that they act. The result is a terrible mess.

The absent father

> ❓ *Where does Jacob settle, and what does he do (33:18-20)?*

It all seems admirable, until we remember that he was meant to return to Bethel, as he had promised (28:18-22). Compromised, partial obedience always eventually leads to misery.

> ❓ *What does Jacob say and do in 34:1-12?*

Here is a father who is physically present but is as good as useless. He is passive and takes no responsibility or action whatsoever.

> ❓ *What fact about Dinah is repeated four times in verses 1-7?*

Pointedly we are told that Jacob's sons are outraged about this, but he expresses no emotion. That he even entertains Hamor and Shechem's proposal is shocking.

Chips off the old block

In verses 13-29, still Jacob says nothing. His sons take over—and reveal that they have learned from Jacob's deceiving ways.

> ❓ *What do they require from Shechem and his men in verses 13-17?*

How shameful to abuse the holy ritual of circumcision.

> ❓ *Before we feel too sorry for Shechem, what do we learn about his motives in verse 18-24?*

Having seized their sister, he now wants to seize all their possessions too (verse 23).

What happens next is shocking. Without godly leadership to restrain it, sin spreads and grows, bringing misery and death.

A glimpse of grace
Re-read Genesis 34:30-31

Again Jacob shows no concern for his poor daughter, but only his own skin. What will the family have to do now? God uses this mess to bring the family back to Bethel, where they should always have settled.

⌄ Apply

> ❓ *Do these events resonate with your own experiences in some way? Please find a trusted, wise Christian to talk to if you need to.*

Read Romans 12:17-19. Pray for yourself or others you know who are struggling not to give in to bitterness and hatred. Pray that God's love and promise of justice will sustain them.

Bible in a year: Ezekiel 37-39 • John 18 v 1-18 ✔

Web wisdom

We are blessed—and cursed—to live in a time when we can respond and reply immediately to people and situations around the globe.

Some people dismiss Scripture as out of date and of no value. How wrong could they be...

Net rules
Read Proverbs 15:1-2, 4

> ❷ *What is the basic point being made in these verses?*
> ❷ *What powerful word pictures are evoked by the adjectives and verbs here?*

It is not hard to find polarising opinions on the internet. In fact, we are told that the algorithms that choose what to include in our Facebook, Twitter or Instagram feeds will naturally prefer posts with "strong opinions". The nature of the medium seems to encourage us to kick back with knee-jerk reactions—on politics, people and religion. But like the best page moderator, these verses give us a set of "best practice" rules for engaging with others.

> ❷ *How would you summarise them?*

It's basic stuff really. Be kind. Stay rooted in the facts, not opinion. And even if someone is harsh and hostile, treat them with gentleness and respect.

···· **TIME OUT** ································
Read 1 Peter 3:16-17

> ❷ *How does this verse encourage us to speak, write and respond to those who attack us for our beliefs?*

Net effect
Re-read Proverbs 15:1-2, 4

> ❷ *What effect will kind, wise words have on the nature of a conversation?*
> ❷ *What will happen if our words are <u>not</u> godly and wise?*

If you want to practise your debating skills, there are plenty of forums where you can have a knockabout slanging match with atheists. But what good does it actually achieve? It is far better to try to establish a proper relationship with someone, where you share about your life, listen to them, ask good questions about what they believe and why they believe, and offer trusted evidence and facts, rather than getting angry or opinionated. We must be Christ-like in our engagement with others, in both everyday conversation and online, if our aim is to bring life, peace and grace.

Web watcher
Read Proverbs 15:3

> ❷ *Why is it important to remember this when you are online in particular?*

◤ Pray

Ask the Lord to help you as you relate well to others, both online and in the flesh. Pray that your web words would be wise.

All change

To move from rejecting God and worshipping idols to worshipping God and working to obey him is as significant as changing your name.

Read Genesis 35:1-8

Now that he is in danger of a revenge attack from the Canaanites, Jacob heads to Bethel at last.

> ❓ *What does Jacob require of his family in the next verses?*

Even the family of God's promises has accumulated foreign gods (idols). The same can be true of Christians. While we say we worship Jesus, we can, in practice, have lots of other "godlets" too—things that we look to and rely on and pursue because deep down we think they will provide what in fact only God can give: whether it's career success to provide us with the respect we long for, or money to give us security, or a relationship that we think will fulfil our deepest longings. Like Jacob's family, we must get rid of these.

> ❓ *How do verses 5-7 encourage us to see that it is worth ridding ourselves of the other things we worship?*

Jacob's family quickly learn that God is able to protect them and provide for them.

Read Genesis 35:9-15

> ❓ *What does "Jacob" mean (see footnote)?*
> ❓ *What does "Israel" mean?*

It's as if God is saying in verses 9-10, *It's time to live out who you are. Stop being Jacob; be Israel. Be who I call you to be. Live out your new identity and destiny.*

This will not be easy. It is a struggle to live with God, and for God. At times it feels like struggling *with* God. That is the life of faith.

God first made promises to fallen humanity in 3:15, and to Abraham's family in 12:1-3.

> ❓ *What is promised in 35:11-13, that wasn't promised to Adam and Eve, or in the initial promises to Abram?*

It's hard to think of a less promising source for God's kings! We should not be surprised, then, when his ultimate, eternal King, descended from Jacob, is born in a shed to an unmarried girl.

☑ Apply

The Bible uses the image of new clothing as a picture of the complete change in identity given to every Christian, and the complete change in behaviour required of every Christian:

Read Ephesians 4:20-24

> ❓ *What attitudes and behaviours do you need to take off?*

Of course, taking off the old clothes is only half of what the Bible requires.

> ❓ *What Spirit-filled attitudes and actions are you particularly aware that you need to put on?*

Pray for God's help in getting rid of the idols and "old clothes", and in putting on the new.

Happily ever after?

Some movies have deliberately unsatisfactory endings, where the loose plot threads are not tied up. Usually it's because they are teeing things up for a lucrative sequel…

This passage tells us about the end of Jacob's pilgrimage, but there is a sense of unfulfilment to it. There is more to come!

The circle of life
Read Genesis 35:16-20

The great joy of God's glorious promises to Jacob in verses 11-12 is followed by great sorrow.

> ❓ *Why would this death have been particularly bitter for Jacob?*

The love of his life is dead, but she has given him another son, Benjamin. Now he has twelve sons.

Unhappy families
Read Genesis 35:21-26

God promised in verse 11 that his descendants would be kings. But who among Jacob's sons is worthy to rule? Already Simeon and Levi have disqualified themselves with their murderous vengeance in chapter 34. Now his eldest, Reuben, shows his unworthiness.

> ❓ *What does he do?*

He's trying to show that he now rules the family (see 2 Samuel 16:20-22). Reuben is unworthy to lead the family, but once again, Jacob proves unwilling to lead it, as he does nothing.

We get another reminder of the mess in this family in Genesis 35:23-26.

> ❓ *How are Jacob's sons listed?*

The family has been divided from the start. Soon enough that split will threaten to tear the family apart for ever.

The best is yet to come
Read Genesis 35:27-29

There is a painful irony in the burying of Isaac at Mamre. In Genesis 18:1 and 10, Mamre was where God promised Abraham that Isaac would be born.

This passage is marked by a nagging sense of unfulfilment. Jacob's family remains dysfunctional, and Isaac dies. Hebrews 11:39-40 reminds us that God's great promises are not focused on everything working out in this life but in the life to come. Like Jacob, we await the day when we will enjoy the full measure of God's promised blessings: not the hope of a happy ending so much as a happy movie that never ends!

> ❓ *In what way do you need to hear this, and feel hope in this, today?*

Pray

Pray for faith to serve and obey God while you look forward to the fulfilment of all his wonderful promises when Christ returns. Take your disappointments and disillusionments with this life and give them up to God, praying that he would help you look forward to the glorious life to come.

Bible in a year: Ezekiel 45-46 · John 19 v 23-42

The other family

Genealogies tend not to be our favourite bits of the Bible at the best of times. But this one is not even about the covenant family of Jacob. So, why include it?

Why waste a whole chapter detailing the offspring of a man who rejected God and turned away from the family of promise?

Seeds of conflict
Read Genesis 36:1-12

We see here how far Esau has fallen. It begins in v 1 with his other name. Throughout the Old Testament, the Edomites were always at war with God's people (2 Samuel 8:13-14; 1 Kings 11:15-16; 2 Kings 14:7; etc.). Obadiah prophesied judgment for their treatment of Israel (read Obadiah v 8-10).

❷ *What are we told about Esau's wives in Genesis 36:2?*

In 26:34-35 we learn that Esau's first two wives were a "source of grief" to his parents. They were Canaanites, likely to draw Esau away from serving the LORD. And while Esau did not know they disapproved (v 8-9) and perhaps they should have told him, he clearly had not asked them for their guidance and wisdom, either over who to marry or how many wives to marry.

Finally, tucked in the middle of 36:12, is another ominous name.

❷ *Can you spot what it is?*

This boy's descendants tried to destroy the Israelites as they journeyed to the promised land (Deuteronomy 25:17-18).

The point being made is this: Esau's lack of

wisdom in marriage set his family and his descendants on a trajectory away from God and towards conflict with God's people.

Seeds of hope
Read Genesis 36:9-30

❷ *How many sons does Esau have? Who else has recently enjoyed the same blessing?*

God does not reject Esau completely. He cares for him and provides a family. Centuries later, in Deuteronomy 23:7, God would tell the Israelites to care for the Edomites, "because they are related to you".

Read Genesis 36:31-43

But still... why such a long genealogy listing all the descendants in detail? It is a hint they have not been written off by God. It gives hope that one day their descendants will come back to God and his people.

It was a hope that was fulfilled in Jesus Christ. Now peoples of all tribes and nations can join God's people. **Read Ephesians 2:13-14, 19-22.** In the gospel those who were once enemies are reconciled at the cross.

▼ Apply

Don't give up hope for those who don't yet trust in Christ. Whether it is members of your own family or people groups far away, don't give up hope. Pray for them. Seek ways of sharing Christ with them.

Swimming lessons

You need swimming lessons before you fall into deep water. The same is true of faith. You need to learn to trust God before you face confusing, difficult circumstances.

The story of Joseph helps us to do that.

The focus of Genesis 37 – 50 is providence: the truth that God is sovereignly at work through people and circumstances to bring about his good purposes. Each chapter will build upon, embed and consolidate this truth. As we see how God works through the story of Joseph, we will learn to trust that God is at work behind the scenes in our lives too, and that nothing can stop his good plans. When your life, or the lives of those you love, is messy, painful or dark, you need a firm grip on this truth, or you will be crippled with doubt and bitterness.

Unhappy families
Read Genesis 37:1-11

> ❓ *What do we learn about Jacob?*
> ❓ *What do we learn about the behaviour and attitudes of Joseph's brothers?*

We don't know whether Joseph's report in verse 2 is fair, but given how his brothers behave in this chapter, it seems likely!

> ❓ *What impression do we get of Joseph?*

He sounds like a spoilt brat! I can't imagine he was popular with anyone other than his doting father, whose indulgent love had ruined him.

Here is a family ruined by favouritism, pride, hatred and jealousy. Here is a warning that sin brings misery. Jacob has failed to root out sin in his own heart and has failed to raise his children in the instruction of the Lord. Now he is beginning to reap the whirlwind.

A divine promise
Re-read Genesis 37:5-11

> ❓ *What is the meaning of Joseph's dreams?*
> ❓ *How does his family respond to them?*

It's not hard to imagine the smug voice and self-satisfied grin as Joseph interrupts family breakfast to tell them all about his dreams.

God's plan for this family comes through a surprising source, but Joseph's dreams reveal what God is going to do in these chapters.

☑ Apply

God promises in Romans 8:28 that "in all things God works for the good of those who love him".

> ❓ *When do you find it hard to trust God's promise that he is at work in your life?*
> ❓ *What difference will it make to remember that, often despite appearances, this verse is true?*

☒ Pray

Pray that as we work through this Joseph narrative, God would deepen your trust in him no matter what you are facing in life.

With brothers like this…

Forget the feel-good family musical. The story of Joseph is about a brutal battle.

In one corner is the God of the Bible and his plan to work through Jacob's family to bring salvation to the world. In the other corner is sin—the sinful failings of Jacob's family, the sinful opposition of others, and behind it all, Satan himself, who will stop at nothing to destroy God's plan. Who will win…?

Satan 1, God 0?

Read Genesis 37:12-20

❓ *What name is repeated three times in these verses?*

This is not a good place for Jacob's family. Last time they were there, in chapter 34, Dinah was raped, and Simeon and Levi slaughtered the town in revenge. It is not surprising that Jacob wanted to check what his sons were up to!

In 3:15, God promised to work through the offspring of Eve to destroy the devil and redeem humanity. He warned that the devil would violently oppose this work—and in Genesis 4 we saw what this might mean as Cain gave in to hatred and killed his brother Abel.

❓ *So why should alarm bells ring as we read 37:4 and 8?*
❓ *What do they now plan to do?*

Satan is at work behind the scenes, seeking to destroy the family of promise—to destroy God's plan to rescue humanity.

Read Genesis 37:21-28

❓ *What do you make of Reuben's conduct here?*
❓ *What thwarts his plan?*

Light in the darkness

God is not mentioned anywhere in these verses, but if we read carefully, we can see his footprints.

Look back through verses 12-28, looking for the two big coincidences. When Joseph arrives in Shechem, a man just happens to find him (v 15) who knows the brothers are heading to Dothan. When the brothers plan to kill Joseph, a caravan of Ishmaelites just happens to pass by (v 25). It's not much at this stage, but it's a hint that God is providentially at work behind the scenes.

As followers of Jesus, we are on one side of a cosmic conflict. Satan is at war with God, so we should expect some opposition and difficulty in this life. But we must hold on to the truth that there is only one God, and he is in control.

Pray

Pray that your trust in God's good rule would not be shaken when evil seems to have the upper hand. Speak to him about specific ways that you are finding this hard at the moment.

It doesn't pay

Every now and then someone dies after climbing into the tiger enclosure at a zoo. "The tigers look so cute," they seem to have thought: "Surely they won't harm me?"

We can be just as blind and foolish when it comes to sin. "It doesn't seem that serious; it's only a little sin after all…" But as we'll see today, sin deceives, sin dehumanises and sin destroys.

Covering up the crime

The brothers have flogged their own brother, a descendant of Isaac, to descendants of Ishmael. But as the camel train and Joseph's wailing cries fade into the distance, they are left with a problem: how do they explain what's happened to their father, who loved Joseph more than all of them put together?

Read Genesis 37:29-33

❷ *What do the brothers do to cover their crime?*

Notice how they describe Joseph in verse 32: not as "our brother" but as "your son". And there is bitter irony here. Years earlier Jacob had wanted his brother out of the way and had deceived his father using… his brother's stolen clothes and a slaughtered goat.

Read Galatians 6:7-8. Heed the warning: when we sow sin, we reap misery.

Sin never pays

Read Genesis 37:34-36

❷ *How does Jacob respond to Joseph's "death"?*

The brothers were jealous of Joseph. They wanted him out of the way. But they do not get the affection their father lavished on Joseph. They just ruin Jacob. Sin never pays what it promises. As Paul teaches in Romans 6:23, "The wages of sin is death". In spite of any short-term pleasure, that is always the long-term pay. How different things are with God: "… but the gift of God is eternal life in Jesus Christ our Lord".

⌄ Apply

❷ *In what ways are you in danger of buying the lie that sin will deliver you happiness? How have you seen in the past that this is not the case?*

The glimmer

It seems that Satan has won. Joseph is as good as dead, and the family is more miserable and divided than ever. But right at the end is a glimmer of light in verse 36—a hint that all is not lost. Joseph has not disappeared from view. The story will continue in Egypt.

⌃ Pray

Pray that God would "lead us not into temptation"—that you and those you love would see through the "sweet" lies of sin and that you would know the goodness and satisfaction of holiness.

Family values

The vast majority of us are raised in households. Each is different—small or large; rich or poor; containing one parent, two parents, or perhaps an extended family.

And we are all shaped by the experience.

In today's verses from Proverbs 15, we'll focus on part of the Bible's recipe for a happy, nurturing household.

Listen to Dad
Read Proverbs 15:5

- ❓ *What situation does the first proverb bring to mind?*
- ❓ *Can you think of any biblical stories where this happens?*
- ❓ *Can you think of any family situations you know of (your own family or others') where this has proved true?*

It is common in popular media and comedy to portray fathers as weak and ineffectual, and mothers as coping and capable (think Fred Flintstone, Homer Simpson, etc). Of course dads (and mums) can be weak, foolish and selfish, but in Scripture, the prime responsibility for the household clearly falls on the father: to lead, to train, to encourage. And when it goes wrong, it can be deeply painful and catastrophic. Think David with his children (2 Samuel 13 – 15); think the prodigal son.

····· **TIME OUT** ·····························
Read Ephesians 6:1-4

- ❓ *How do the responsibilities outlined here for both fathers and children build on what we have read in Proverbs?*

Pray for your own family and others you know, that they would live this way.

Money counts
Read Proverbs 15:6, 16-17, 27

- ❓ *What perspectives do each of these proverbs give us on how money and wealth is valued in a household?*
- ❓ *Imagine being invited to eat with the two families in verse 17. What would dinner be like? What would you say to them as you left?*
- ❓ *What really matters in a healthy home?*

The Lord Jesus is clear that we cannot serve both God and money (see Matthew 6:24). We need to constantly remind ourselves that what really counts is a healthy relationship with God and genuine love. When these are in place, then a happy family is the result.

⌄ Apply

- ❓ *How were you taught to think about money as a child?*
- ❓ *If you have children living with you, what values are you passing on to them about the relative value of money?*

⌃ Pray

Thank God for the aspects of your upbringing that have shaped you positively. Pray for your own family, or families in your church, to have wisdom to apply these verses well.

Judah and Tamar

This is a truly shocking story in which Judah's only defence for sleeping with his daughter-in-law is that he thought she was a prostitute.

What good can come from a man like this, and what point is there in recording his awful story? Because it shows us that though sin ruins, God redeems. The gospel can shine in this kind of darkness—and maybe you or someone you know desperately needs to hear that today.

A bad start
Read Genesis 38:1-11

Before we see how Joseph behaves in slavery, we see what his brother Judah gets up to in freedom. He descends (spiritually as well as geographically) and follows Uncle Esau by marrying a Canaanite. His sons do not turn out well.

> ❷ *Why does Judah refuse to let Tamar marry his third son, Shelah?*

What a superstitious fool! His sons died because of their sin, not because of some problem with Tamar. Judah's reasoning is like someone saying, "I'm selling this wretched car, because every time I drive it I get a speeding ticket."

It gets worse

Judah has been unfaithful, superstitious and unkind. Then he gets worse.
Read Genesis 38:12-26

> ❷ *What does he do in verses 12-19?*

In chapter 37, Judah deceived Jacob with a goat and some personal possessions (just as Jacob had deceived Isaac a generation before). Now Judah is deceived, and it involves... a goat and some personal possessions.

Judah is happy to have sex with a prostitute.

> ❷ *But how does he respond when Tamar is accused of prostitution (v 24)?*
> ❷ *What must it have been tempting for Judah to do in verses 25-26?*
> ❷ *What does he do?*

This is the beginning of his rise.

Tamar's son
Read Genesis 38:27-30

These are, in one sense, the most shocking verses in the chapter: maybe not on first reading—but **read Matthew 1:3**. Jesus is descended from a baby born because a lustful hypocrite mistook his daughter-in-law for a prostitute.

Since God's Son was born into a family like that, then never think that you are too sinful, too filthy or too abused to be adopted into God's family through Jesus Christ. And since God's Son was born into a family like that, then never doubt that God can be at work in your family and your life. Here is wonderful assurance that our circumstances can never be too messy for God to be gloriously involved in. This is grace, and here is hope.

How does that hope speak to you today?

Joseph and Mrs Potiphar

How do you expect God to treat you if you sacrificially serve him and resist temptation, even when the pressure is extreme? Joseph's reward is a seven-year stretch in prison.

Put in charge
Read Genesis 39:1-6

❷ *What name is God given repeatedly in these verses?*

This name essentially means "the God who made promises to Abraham and his descendants—and kept every one of them". The author is saying that the faithful, promise-keeping God was looking out for Joseph.

❷ *What is the result of this?*

Come to bed!
Read Genesis 39:6-20

❷ *How is Joseph described?*

The Bible doesn't often give personal descriptions, but Joseph's good looks change the course of his life.

❷ *How does Joseph respond to Mrs Potiphar's temptations?*
❷ *What happens to Joseph?*

One wonders whether Potiphar was less than fully convinced by his wife's story. That would explain why Joseph goes to jail, not the gallows.

Put in charge
Read Genesis 39:20-23

❷ *What similarities can you see with verses 1-6?*

It might seem odd to read that the LORD is with Joseph, when Joseph has been falsely accused and thrown from slavery into prison. But God is with him, and again, Joseph is prospering because of that.

So what is God up to? Far more than Joseph can have realised! First, God is humbling Joseph: refining his character so he is ready for the role God has planned for him. He will leave prison very different to the spoiled brat who taunted his brothers (37:5-9).

Second, when we zoom out and see this chapter in the context of Genesis and indeed the whole Bible story, we see that God is using Joseph's actions to preserve the promised family line into which the Messiah will be born. More on that to come...

But Joseph, of course, knows none of that at this point. He just knows that obeying God is the right thing to do.

✔ Apply

God doesn't tell us what our costly obedience will achieve. But as we read the account of Joseph, we should be encouraged to keep fighting sin, for who knows what good God might work through our costly, seemingly unseen obedience?

❷ *How does that encourage you, and challenge you, today?*

Pray for faith to believe that it is worthwhile obeying God even when it costs you deeply.

When tempted, resist

Genesis 39 is far more than a lesson in resisting temptation—but nevertheless, Joseph's example gives us some key ways to deal with it.

Read Genesis 39:1-23

Joseph is a slave with no prospect of freedom or marriage. It would have been easy to justify sleeping with Potiphar's wife: *After all, don't I deserve to have my desires fulfilled? She's not happy in her marriage, so there's no real harm, is there?*

How does he find the strength to resist?

He is ready for it. Look at his response in verses 8-9. He didn't think that up on the spur of the moment! It is clear that he has noticed the flirtatious signals and has prayed and prepared.

He sees sin as sin. The first step towards disobedience is redefinition. We rename dishonesty as "accentuating the positive on my resumé'. We call lustful flirtation "office banter". We describe gossip as "sharing concerns". But Joseph is clear. This is a sin against God.

He flees rather than fights. Many of us stand firm when tempted the first time, but take no steps to prevent the situation recurring— and then we fall down when the temptation comes again and again and again. Joseph, though, is not complacent and doesn't over-estimate his ability to resist. He won't even go near Potiphar's wife (v 10).

He values God's honour over earthly comfort. He must have known that her grabbing his coat might end badly. But what matters to him is getting away from temptation. He would rather suffer than sin.

He obeys for God's sake, not because he thinks he'll be rewarded.

❷ *What happens to Joseph as a result of obeying God (v 13-23)?*
❷ *How does he then behave in prison?*

This is the acid test: how do we respond when obeying God doesn't "work"? How do we respond when we refuse to give in to sexual temptation, but God doesn't then reward us with a spouse? How do we respond when we give generously and faithfully, but then we lose our job and can't find another?

If deep down we only obey God because we think he'll reward us in this life, then we will never last long. God will richly reward, but his rewards are focused on the next life, not this one.

Jesus, the greater Joseph, resisted temptation every second of every minute of every day of his whole life. And "because he himself suffered when he was tempted, he is able to help those who are being tempted" (Hebrews 2:18).

⌄ Apply

❷ *In what ways are you regularly tempted to sin? In what ways are you regularly giving in? Take time to answer.*
❷ *What would it look like to respond to those temptations in the way Joseph did?*

Commit to actually doing this. Then ask Jesus to help you, in those moments, to resist and obey.

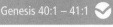
The story is not over

It is easy to put life, and faithfulness, on hold when things are hard. It's easy to focus on "me and my disappointments", and stop seeing and serving the needs of others.

Serving while suffering

Read Genesis 40:1-4

- ❓ *What role does Joseph seem to have in prison?*
- ❓ *Why might this be surprising?*

In spite of all that Joseph has been through, he continues to serve others and take responsibility. That is faith—trusting and serving when we don't know what God is doing or whether he will change our circumstances.

Dreaming of… what?

Read Genesis 40:5-22

Joseph is caring enough to notice that the cupbearer and the baker have not slept well.

- ❓ *What is the cause?*
- ❓ *Why is Joseph confident that he can help them?*

Still here

Joseph had been in prison for almost five years when he helped Pharaoh's cupbearer (see 37:2 and 41:46). But now at last he has a friend who has the ear of the king. At last his injustice will be rectified, and he will be released. You can imagine him waking up excited the day after the cupbearer is restored. But no message came from the palace that day. Or the next day. Or the one after that.

Read Genesis 40:23 – 41:1

- ❓ *Why does nothing change (40:23)?*
- ❓ *How long is it before things do change (41:1)?*

What were you doing two years ago? What have you done since? It's a long time. God's ways can seem slow—painfully slow at times. But God is often more like a glacier than a wind. A strong wind can seem impressive as it makes the trees moan and sway. By contrast, stand on top of a glacier, and it seems that nothing is happening. But the slow, imperceptible movement of a glacier can gouge valleys out of rock! God is at work in Joseph—slowly grinding down sin and building holiness in him, and making sure he is in the right place at the right time to fulfil God's great plans for his people.

We need to learn not to judge things until the story is complete. And the story is not complete until Jesus returns, restores his people, brings justice and wipes our tears away. So often we look at the circumstances of our lives and think God has forgotten us or that everything is beyond hope. The long, slow story of Joseph teaches us to trust and wait in the darkness.

⌃ Pray

Pray that you will trust that God is at work even when it seems that nothing is happening, even when it feels that your hopes are raised only to be dashed again and again.

From glacier to volcano

God's work in Joseph has progressed like a glacier—moving imperceptibly for 13 long, painful years. But when the time is right, the glacier becomes a volcano.

Now Joseph, his character refined and prepared, erupts from the depths of hopelessness to the very summit of power and prestige.

More strange dreams
Read Genesis 41:1-14

The strange dreams have spread from the prison to the palace.

> ❓ *Where does Pharaoh turn for help with his perplexing dreams?*

Amid the furrowed brows and blank stares of the wise men, the butler feels a sharp pang of guilt and tells Pharaoh about Joseph.

> ❓ *What happens next?*

Look at the contrast in timing in verses 1 and 14: "When two full years had passed ... he was quickly brought". God often works slowly—but when he is ready, he can transform things in a moment.

God will do it
Read Genesis 41:15-32

> ❓ *How much credit does Joseph take for his ability to interpret dreams?*

The dream is repeated in verses 17-24, to build up the tension. What on earth can it mean?

> ❓ *What is Joseph's explanation for the dream coming in two forms (v 32)?*

After (or perhaps, partly *because of*) all Joseph has been through, he still knows who God is—that God is good, and God is sovereign. Joseph's circumstances have been changeable and uncertain—the God who moves behind them is neither.

Prison to palace
Read Genesis 41:33-40

> ❓ *What position does Pharaoh appoint Joseph to?*

That is quite the meteoric rise!

There is no such thing as hopelessness when God is involved. He can transform even the darkest mess in the briefest instant. He does it here with Joseph. He did it supremely with Jesus: taking him from cursed death and cold tomb to resurrection glory in an instant! We can, and must, trust this God as we face the chronic struggles that so easily breed hopelessness. Even if he does not change our circumstances now, one day we too will go from dead and buried to eternally alive in paradise!

🔼 Pray

> ❓ *What tempts you to feel hopeless?*

Pray that God would sustain your faith in his resurrection power as you pray about "hopeless" situations.

> ❓ *Who could you share this with today, to encourage them to cling to hope?*

Looking up

In these verses we see how God brings rich blessing after great hardship.

A royal makeover

Read Genesis 41:41-45

❓ *How is everything that Joseph lost now replaced by something greater? (Don't look down at the answer below before answering it from the passage!)*

His rich robe was torn off him by his brothers. His slave's robe was torn off him by Potiphar's wife. Now the king of Egypt puts a new, royal robe on him and adorns him with a gold chain. Joseph refused to enjoy sex when it would have meant committing adultery. Now he is given a wife. It is just a hint pointing towards Jesus. He voluntarily humbled himself, not just to slavery and prison but to death on a cross. And then his Father exalted him to the highest place, not in Egypt but over the cosmos: **read Philippians 2:5-11.**

Remember the source

Read Genesis 41:46-76

❓ *What happens in verses 46-49 and then in verses 53-56?*

So why do we get the domestic interruption about births and baby names?

❓ *What do the names Joseph gives to his children mean, and why does Joseph choose those names (v 50-52)?*

Joseph is acknowledging the hand of God in his blessings. He may have been told to marry the daughter of a priest to the Egyptian gods, but he will honour the God who he knows has made him fruitful after he led him through suffering.

As an aside, it's interesting to note what Joseph *doesn't* receive between the ages of 17 and 30. He receives no teaching. The arrogant brat of chapter 37 already knew all he needed. But it took years of suffering for that teaching to bear fruit in his life, so that he grew into the godly leader of chapter 41 who was so quick to acknowledge that it was God who had given him all he had and had put him where he was.

So it should be for us. If God was able to work such deep, rich good in the life of Joseph through his suffering, how can we fail to trust that he is at work through our suffering too? If God rewarded Joseph so richly after his trials, how can we fail to trust that he will reward us too? "Our light and momentary troubles are achieving for us an eternal glory that far outweighs them all" (2 Corinthians 4:17).

⌄ Apply

❓ *How should the prospect of future glory shape the way you look at your day—its ups and its downs—today?*
❓ *When was the last time you praised God for the eternity he has set before you, and for the blessings he has given you now?*

Do so now!

What God hates

Ask a random person in the street what they think of religious people, and it won't be long before you hear the word "hypocrites". They have a point.

But what they perhaps don't realise is that God is just as angry about religious hypocrisy as they are.

God hates...

Read Proverbs 15:8-10

- ❓ *What do the first half of each of these three proverbs tell us about God's reaction to evil—wherever he finds it?*
- ❓ *What will his response be to wickedness (v 10a)?*
- ❓ *What distinction does God make between those who seem to obey God (v 8a) and those who clearly do not?*

What is remarkable is that there is *no distinction at all*. Many people think that God is appeased by an occasional sacrifice—visiting church on high days and holy days; a gift to charity or for the church roof; an act of selfless kindness. But without an underlying godliness and a willingness to change (v 10), these sacrifices actually only serve to stoke up God's anger towards us.

⌄ Apply

We may not be outwardly living a life that anyone might conceivably call "wicked", but we must beware of two inward attitudes that God hates and will punish: insincere religion (v 8a) and hard-heartedness (v 10b).

Search your heart for these traits now, and talk to God about what you find there.

❓ *What would need to change for your faith to be described as sincere and wholehearted?*

God loves...

Re-read Proverbs 15:9

- ❓ *What does God love?*
- ❓ *What do you think "pursuing righteousness" actually means?*

God hears...

Read Proverbs 15:8, 29

- ❓ *What kind of prayers does God love to listen to?*
- ❓ *How can we be confident that God will hear and answer our prayers?*

⌄ Apply

- ❓ *Do these verses fill you with confidence, or with fear that your prayers won't be heard? Why is that?*
- ❓ *If "fear", how do 2 Corinthians 5:21 and Hebrews 4:16 help with that fear?*

⌃ Pray

Even if our sanctification (progress to holiness) leaves much to be desired, we are counted righteous if we are in Christ. So we can come before God with confidence and boldness. Do that now, and ask him to work in you, to the glory of his Son Jesus.

Meanwhile, in Canaan…

I love a good heist movie. I love the meticulous planning, in which the various pieces come together to do the seemingly impossible. That is what happens in Genesis 42 – 45.

Joseph has never had it so good. The same cannot be said for his brothers...

Canaan to Egypt
Read Genesis 42:1-5

❓ *How are Joseph's family doing back in Canaan?*

They face starvation, and Jacob's poisonous favouritism is now being focused on Joseph's only full brother, Benjamin.

Read Genesis 42:6-20

Joseph is the prime minister of all Egypt, and yet he happens to be in the right place to see his brothers' arrival after their week long trudge for food.

❓ *Why might verse 6 have caused Joseph to remember his dreams (see 37:7)?*
❓ *What does Joseph do to unsettle and test his brothers?*

The family can never be truly reconciled unless the brothers are truly repentant. So Joseph applies all his planning skills to test his brothers. Like God, he puts them through a trial for their good. The result will be that the family of promise is saved from famine and reconciled, and the next phase of God's great plan of salvation can be fulfilled.

Read Genesis 42:21-24

❓ *How do Joseph's brothers respond to his accusations?*

❓ *Why do you think this makes Joseph weep?*

After 20 years, here are his brothers expressing remorse for their treatment of Joseph. It must have been overwhelming!

Egypt to Canaan
Read Genesis 42:25-38

❓ *What does Joseph do to his brothers when they leave?*
❓ *When they discover it, who do they mention, for the very first time (v 28)?*
❓ *How does Jacob respond to what has happened?*
❓ *Why might his words in verse 36 have been painful to them?*

The brothers were willing to sell Joseph for 30 shekels. Will they leave Simeon now they have their money and the food they need? He is their full brother, but will their greed get the better of them?

☑ Apply

God afflicts Jacob's family with a famine for their good. Without this famine, the family could never have been reconciled. We must learn to do what the seventeenth-century Puritans called "kissing the rod"—to trust that God never allows us to suffer without working good in our lives from it.

❓ *How does this truth need to shape your emotions and reactions today?*

Enjoying what we have

Throughout these chapters the brothers react to events in front of them but are ignorant of the purposes behind them. It is a picture of our lives.

We are like these brothers: often fearful, confused and overwhelmed. God is like a greater Joseph: calmly working out his good plans for our ultimate blessing.

Dilemma

The trolley problem is an ethical dilemma in which a trolley (tram) is going to plough into a group of people. The controller can divert it onto another track, but her only child is on that track. Will she sacrifice her one child to save lots of people she does not love?

Read Genesis 43:1-14

❓ *What dilemma does Jacob face?*

Throughout his married life he has ruined his family with his favouritism—Rachel over Leah, and then Rachel's sons, Joseph and Benjamin, over Leah's children.

Finally, in verses 11-14, Jacob is willing to put the needs of the family ahead of his favouritism. God is digging up some of the deep-rooted sins that Jacob has nurtured for decades. It is painful, but it is for his good. Joseph has planned to test his brothers. But as ever, God has even greater plans. He is also at work in Jacob.

❓ *How does Judah begin to demonstrate the godly character necessary for a leader in these verses? (Look at the contrast with Reuben in 42:37.)*

Temptation
Read Genesis 43:15-34

The famine presented Joseph with the opportunity to test his brothers. Now he will test them with a feast!

❓ *What is their fear (v 15-18)?*
❓ *How does the steward reassure them (v 23-24)?*

Notice how God is increasingly mentioned in the speeches.

❓ *How does Joseph respond to the news from home (v 26-30)?*
❓ *What unexpected thing does Joseph do to test the brothers at dinner?*
❓ *How do Joseph's brothers respond to Benjamin's special treatment?*
❓ *How might we expect them to have responded, given what has gone on before?*

They are surprised, but they are not bitter. They do not grumble but enjoy the feast before them.

☑ Apply

❓ *What do you tend to grumble about? What do you envy?*
❓ *What would you enjoy more if you weren't busy thinking about what you don't have or worrying about the future?*
❓ *How would memorising Romans 8:28 help you?*

In place of the boy

Joseph has been building towards a final test to see whether his brothers have really changed. Will they protect their father's favoured son when their lives are at stake?

An expensive souvenir

Read Genesis 44:1-13

❓ *What did Joseph do, and how do you think the brothers would have felt?*

Can you imagine the rising tension as the steward searched each of the 11 sacks?!

In chapter 37 they tore Joseph's robe to cover their wicked sale of him. Now (44:13) they tear their own robes in sorrow at the fate of their youngest brother.

Sacrificial leadership

Read Genesis 44:14-34

❓ *Which brother steps up to lead at this point?*

❓ *Why do you think he confesses their guilt?*

He sees this as rightful justice for their unpunished crime against Joseph all those years ago.

❓ *How does Joseph sharpen the test of his brothers?*

❓ *What is the great concern of Judah in these verses?*

Judah's words are strikingly tender and kind. It cannot have been easy to say the words in verses 27-29, knowing that he too was a son of Jacob, that his mother Leah too was a wife for Jacob. He cares more about honouring the father who never fully loved

him than for his own welfare.

❓ *What offer does Judah make?*

❓ *How does this chapter prove that Joseph's brothers are truly repentant?*

Here is another glorious hint of Jesus. Joseph has been like Jesus in many ways in these chapters—but now it is Judah who shines a light on what Jesus will one day do. He is willing to take the place of his brother and suffer the punishment due to him, so that the "guilty" one might be restored to his father.

Of course, Benjamin was innocent of the charge again him. You and I are not. *We are true Benjamins, and Jesus is the greater Judah.* We have a brother who took our place and bore our punishment in order to bring us safely home to our Father, who loves us—and him.

🔺 Pray

Spend time in prayer confessing sin and thanking Jesus that he willingly took your place and punishment so that you could be restored to your heavenly Father.

🔻 Apply

❓ *If you are in leadership of any kind—home, workplace, church, somewhere else—how does Judah here show you the way to conduct yourself in that role?*

From carbon to diamond

Do you know what the difference is between a lump of coal and a dazzling diamond (other than a few thousand pounds in value!)? Pressure.

Under great pressure the carbon that might otherwise be coal becomes a diamond.

In spiritual terms, this is what has been happening in Jacob's family. God has put this family under intense pressure, and now we see the diamond he has created.

Good through evil
Read Genesis 45:1-15

> ❷ *What's the most emotionally overwhelming experience you have had?*

Jacob's brothers have passed the test. They were willing to sacrifice themselves to save Benjamin for the sake of their father.

> ❷ *How does Joseph respond in verses 1-2?*

After all he's been through, it's no wonder he cannot contain his emotions!

Verses 4-7 are the theological key to the previous eight chapters. Joseph has been torn away from his family, sold into slavery, falsely accused and thrown into prison.

> ❷ *How might someone respond when finally they have the opportunity for revenge?*
> ❷ *What two truths does Joseph see that enable him not to be bitter?*

Who is responsible for Joseph being sent to Egypt? Look at verse 8. Joseph can see that, behind it all, God was using his brothers' wickedness to achieve his good purposes.

Family fortunes
Read Genesis 45:16-28

> ❷ *How does Pharaoh respond to the news?*
> ❷ *Why might these verses sound ironic to those who have read the book of Exodus?*
> ❷ *Why do you think Joseph gives his brothers the command in verse 24?*

He is no fool. On the week-long journey back home, it would be easy for the brothers to bicker and indulge in "I told you so" arguments about their past sins!

> ❷ *How does Jacob respond?*

Jacob will not be the only person in the Bible to react like this when told that someone he thought was dead is now alive and has been raised up to rule. **Scan-read John 20:1-31.** But it was still true that Jacob's son was alive. Eventually the evidence convinced Jacob, just as the evidence for Jesus' resurrection convinced the disciples.

☑ Apply

> ❷ *How do the truths of verses 7-8 help us when we face painful or bewildering circumstances?*
> ❷ *How should you pray differently in life's hard seasons because of these verses?*

⌃ Pray

Apply those truths to your life, your family and your church as you pray.

Bible in a year: 1 Samuel 30-31 • 1 Timothy 4

I will go with you

Have you had that unsettling experience when you know you should be heading one way but the satnav tells you to go in the opposite direction?

Having finally settled in the promised land a few years previously, Jacob is about to take his family to Egypt. Surely that is the wrong direction?!

Fear not

Read Genesis 46:1-4

Beersheba is on the edge of the promised land.

> ❷ *What does God do when Jacob gets there?*
> ❷ *Why might Jacob need this reassurance?*

Each time Jacob has had to make a significant journey, God has assured him of his presence (28:10-15; 32:1-2).

> ❷ *What does God promise to him?*

Egypt will not be the final destiny of God's people; it will be the "womb" in which Jacob's family grows into the nation of Israel.

···· TIMEOUT ····································

Hebrews 1:1-3 shows that God does not tend to guide us today in this way with dreams. He has given us all we need in his word (2 Timothy 3:16-17). Don't look for a dream when you have a decision to make. Study God's word, pray to him and seek counsel from others. Then do what seems right and wise, entrusting yourself to his providential care. Like Jacob, though, we never need to fear when we are acting in obedience to God's word!

Unbreakable promises

Read Genesis 46:5-27

> ❷ *Who goes down to Egypt (v 5-7)?*

Finally, the family is reunited. God has lost none of those he promised to hold.

As we read the list of strange names that follows, we are reminded that God doesn't just save groups of people—he saves individuals. If you trust in Jesus, God has called you, and he knows your name (John 10:3; Philippians 4:3).

In the Bible some numbers are significant (see Revelation!). Seven and ten both imply completeness. God has begun to fulfil his promise to give descendants to Abraham. By the time they leave Egypt 400 years later, there will be too many to name. The family will be a nation, just as God promised (Genesis 35:11; 46:3).

❱ Apply

Haven't we already heard lots about God fulfilling promises? Yes. But God thinks it is such an important lesson that he repeats it often in Scripture.

> ❷ *Which promises are you struggling to believe at the moment?*
> ❷ *How does seeing God's promise-keeping record in the past help you trust him today?*

Bible in a year: 2 Samuel 1-2 • 1 Timothy 5

A dangerous place

Where's the most dangerous nation for Christians? Surely those where there's persecution. But in most of the places where the church is declining, it faces no persecution.

Instead, there is the temptation to compromise: to become just like the rest of society. Joseph acts to preserve his family from this very danger.

Reunited
Read Genesis 46:28-30

❓ *Almost every speech Jacob makes is about death—how does he respond to meeting Joseph (v 30)?*

Perhaps we should hear an echo of another old man who says, *Now I'm ready to die* when he meets the one who is the ultimate Saviour of the world—**read Luke 2:29**.

Settling down
Read Genesis 46:31 – 47:6

❓ *What is Joseph's plan, and what motivates it?*

Joseph tells his brothers to be straight and honest with Pharaoh—a novel policy for Jacob's family! He hopes that because the Egyptians despise shepherds, they will let the Israelites keep to themselves.

❓ *How well does it work?*

Once again Joseph's skill enables him to preserve his family from danger. In Canaan, the family kept getting into trouble when they got involved with the Canaanites around them. In Egypt they will be able to flourish in isolation from the Egyptians.

For us, the separation God calls us to is not physical, but it is real. As the old saying puts it, we are to be in the world but not of it. Paul urges us in Romans 12:2, "Do not be conformed to the pattern of this world, but be transformed by the renewing of your mind". We are to be separate in the way we think and behave, even as we are present in the world, seeking to know and serve and love those around us.

Jacob and the Pharaoh
Read Genesis 47:7-12

Can you imagine the scene as old famine-starved Jacob shuffles in to meet the dazzling Pharaoh?

❓ *So what is strange about who says what to whom in verse 10?*

In spite of appearances, Jacob is the greater—he is the one with the blessing to impart. Again and again we see in the Bible that God's power is seen through what looks weak and feeble by human standards.

☑ Apply

❓ *In which areas of life might you be in danger of conforming to the thinking and values of this world?*
❓ *How can you ensure that your attitudes and values are shaped by God each day?*

Heart religion

What goes on in your heart and mind when you are not focused on a specific task? In today's verses, our inner selves are put under the microscope.

An open book
Read Proverbs 15:11-15

- ❓ What is being said about our hearts here? Try to sum up the essence of what is being said in each verse.
- ❓ Why might people imagine that the thoughts of our hearts are opaque to God?
- ❓ Do you find verse 11 unsettling or encouraging? Why?
- ❓ Do you think verse 13 is always true?

People have different temperaments. Some people have a naturally "cheerful heart" (v 15). Others have a downbeat demeanour. But God sees our hearts and knows what goes on deep down—we are all an open book to him. In the "privacy" of our minds, we imagine that our thoughts are just that: private. They are not. This should bring both fear and joy to a Christian. God knows what is really going on. And yet he still loves, embraces and accepts us—because of Christ. That strips away any prideful pretensions we may have. We can fool others—even ourselves—but *never* the Lord. But wonderfully, we don't need to.

Heart words
Read Proverbs 15:18, 26

- ❓ Which category of verse 18 would you put yourself in?
- ❓ Have you had experience of the outcomes it describes?

- ❓ Why do you think verse 26 juxtaposes thoughts with words? What's the connection?

Proverbs, and the rest of the Bible, regularly makes a connection between what is in our hearts and what comes out of our mouths. The tongue reveals what is going on inside.

Hearty appetites
Read Proverbs 15:30, 33

- ❓ What additional perspective is offered by verse 30 to what we have read so far?
- ❓ How does verse 33 sum up what we have read in this chapter about our hearts?

The traffic isn't just one way—words revealing what is in our hearts. There are things that go into us from the outside that affect us. When we look at what is pure and good and of eternal value, we change inside. And hearing good news can be transformative for us. When we hear the good news of Jesus, even weary old bones are energised—it "brings joy to the heart". So we bless and enrich others as we speak gospel truth to both Christians and non-Christians.

⌃ Pray

Ask God to give you a heart that rightly fears him and is humble before him.

And ask the Lord to refresh and renew your own heart deep down.

Glimmers of Jesus

As we get into these final chapters, we see God tie up lots of the loose ends. But things that happen here also point forward to the climax of the Bible—the coming of Jesus.

Saving the world

Read Genesis 47:13-26

❓ *Where is the famine, and how serious is it (v 13-17)?*

❓ *What happens as the famine progresses in verses 18-26?*

How do you feel about what Joseph does here? This is not an endorsement of colonial slavery. The people voluntarily sell themselves and will be able to buy freedom when the rains return. Don't miss how they view the arrangement in verse 25. The Egyptians become Joseph's bond-servants voluntarily for their salvation. That is very different from Pharaoh enslaving the Israelites in Exodus to destroy them.

Joseph has been raised up by God to save people from all nations. Does that remind you of anyone?!

Preserving the promise

Read Genesis 47:27-31

❓ *How do the Israelites fare during this time?*

God is able to make his people flourish. It's no surprise then to find that when God comes to earth, he can feed a hungry crowd in the wilderness (Mark 6:30-44).

Can you remember how long Jacob lived with Joseph in Canaan? That's right, 17 years (Genesis 37:2). The end will match the

beginning. God is tying up the loose ends.

❓ *What does Jacob ask Joseph to do in 47:29-31?*

❓ *Why does this matter to Jacob?*

Canaan, not Egypt, is the land of promise. That is where Jacob knows his future lies.

The greater story

God raises Joseph up to preserve the family of promise (45:7) from dying in the famine, from tearing itself apart through favouritism and hatred, and from being assimilated into pagan Egyptian culture.

Many generations later another Joseph would be born to a man named Jacob. He too would have two dreams from God which would lead him to preserve the family of promise, so that the Messiah would be born (Matthew 1:18-25; 2:13-15). How rich and deep are the layers of God's word! There is always more to discover, to his praise and glory.

⌃ Pray

Praise God for how rich his plan of salvation is. Pray that as you see the tying up of loose ends and the shadows of what is to come, your trust in God's ability to work his good purposes would deepen, and your awe at his glorious ways revealed in his word would grow.

Pass it on

Do you have any precious family heirlooms that are passed down through generations? Jacob had a wonderful heirloom to bequeath: the blessings and promises of God.

Passing on the promise
Read Genesis 48:1-7

Jacob's been talking about dying for 12 chapters and 30 years. Finally, he really is on his deathbed. As Jacob comes to the end of his life, he calls for Joseph before he gathers the rest of his sons in chapter 49.

> ❷ *What does he tell Joseph about when he sees him?*

The most precious thing he has—the most important thing to pass on to his children—is the promise of God, first given to Abraham, which will run down through the generations until it is fulfilled in Jesus Christ (see 2 Corinthians 1:20).

This is true for us too. We have nothing more precious in our possession than the promise of salvation in Jesus. And we have no task more important than to pass it on.

> ❷ *Who are you seeking to share the gospel with at the moment?*
> ❷ *If you have children living at home, how are you proactively prioritising passing on this precious promise?*

God's modus operandi
Read Genesis 48:8-14

As we read the Old Testament, we see that God works in consistent ways. Some familiar patterns reappear here.

> ❷ *Can you spot the links between Jacob's blessing of Joseph's children and Isaac's blessing of Jacob in Genesis 27?*

An old man whose eyes are failing, a kiss, and the younger son taking the blessing due to the firstborn! This is not just family history repeating itself. This is a sign that divine history—salvation history—is progressing.

God's promises and plan flow through the most unlikely of humans: childless women like Sarah, younger brothers like Jacob, despised foreigners like Tamar and hopeless sinners like Judah. It should be no surprise then that eternal life comes to us through a man who was put to death! Always God acts in ways that make it clear that the only explanation is the reality and might of God.

Past, present, future
Read Genesis 48:15-22

> ❷ *How does Jacob's blessing look back to God's faithfulness in the past and forward to what is to come?*
> ❷ *How confident is Jacob that God will fulfil his promise and bring his descendants back to the land of Canaan?*

⌃ Pray

Pray for those you are seeking to share the gospel with. Pray that you would have the same confidence in the gospel promise as Jacob demonstrates in this chapter!

Lion King

We've seen how disastrous it was when Jacob failed to lead his family. And as Jacob's family grow into a nation, they will need a leader.

So, on his deathbed, the old man blesses his sons and appoints one of them to lead the family. But who will it be?

Before you read the passage, it's worth underlining that this is prophecy, not prediction. Jacob is not making an educated guess about the future based on what he's observed about the character of his boys. He is speaking God's prophetic words. In the beginning, God's word created the physical universe. So now the future history of Israel will take shape in obedience to God's word.

The future king
Read Genesis 49:1-7

❷ *Why will none of Jacob's first three sons produce the leaders of Israel (v 4-6— think back to events that we've seen previously in Genesis)?*

Read Genesis 49:8-12

❷ *What does Jacob prophesy Judah's role will be in terms of the family, the nation and the world?*

But Judah, like his older brothers, has been far from sinless (see chapter 38)! Yet God has saved him by grace, and that grace has transformed Judah. He is the one who behaved like a leader when he offered to sacrifice himself in the place of Benjamin (44:18-34).

So, the promise is made: the kings of Israel will come from the tribe of Judah, until a king comes from this tribe who rules not just Judah but the nations too.

Of course, this prophecy points beyond any of the kings who reigned in Jerusalem. Another king would come, who rode on a donkey and whose resurrection elevated him over all peoples (Matthew 28:18). **Read Revelation 5:5.** Jesus is the lion of Judah, the King that God's people need.

True riches
Read Genesis 49:13-28

❷ *What does Jacob say about Joseph?*
❷ *What is more valuable than worldly riches, according to verse 26?*

···· **TIME OUT** ··

Some of the prophecies can be tied to specific things that happen in Israel's history. See if you can do so. (You may want to refer to a Study Bible.)

☑ Apply

Again we're reminded that nothing you can receive from your parents or pass on to your children is as valuable as the blessings of God found in the Lord Jesus.

❷ *How are you seeking to pass these riches on to others?*
❷ *Does your attitude towards worldly wealth suggest you truly believe or disbelieve the truth of verse 26?*

A good death

The word "cemetery" comes from the Greek word for "put to sleep"—and if we trust in Christ, death is not the end; it is just a form of sleep. Bear that in mind as you read.

A God-centred funeral
Read Genesis 49:29-33

> ❓ *Have you ever thought about what you want done with your body when you die?*
> ❓ *What did Jacob ask for, and why was this so important to him?*

For all his ups and downs, Jacob finishes strongly, declaring his trust in God's promises by asking for his body to be buried in the promised land. He entrusts his body and his future to God's promises.

A pagan embalming
Read Genesis 50:1-3

> ❓ *What happens to Jacob's body in these verses?*

A girl I know was worried that the soul of her Christian grandmother might be in jeopardy because the rest of the family insisted on a Buddhist funeral. Similarly, a number of people have said to me that they don't want to be cremated because this might make resurrection impossible.

Thankfully the Bible is clear: "Jesus died and rose again, and so we believe that God will bring with Jesus those who have fallen asleep in him" (1 Thessalonians 4:14). There is no suggestion that pagan embalming or Buddhist burial or cremation can keep us from resurrection in Christ.

Grief with hope
Read Genesis 50:4-14

> ❓ *How do Joseph and his brothers respond to Jacob's death?*

Great hope does not mean there is no grief.

Paul displays a healthy attitude in 1 Thessalonians 4:13: Christians grieve but not as those "who have no hope". Jacob is buried in the only part of the promised land which his family owns. He is buried in hope.

What might it look like for us to be buried in hope? It is not that our bones will be laid in a particular patch of ground. It is that we die trusting in the promises of Jesus Christ (Hebrews 11:39-40). My parents engraved my brother's gravestone with the words "With Christ, which is better by far."

🔼 Pray

Few things rock our faith so much as death—whether it is the searing wrench of losing a loved one or the dark terror of facing our own death. Read through 1 Thessalonians 4:13-18 to reinforce your faith in Jesus as the resurrection and the life.

Then pray that you would trust God even in the face of death, and that he would help you as you seek to share that hope with others.

Providence is wonderful

Few of us understand how a 400-tonne plane is able to fly. But we see them flying so often that we trust that it's safe to get on board. God's providence is like that.

We struggle to understand the theological principles, so God gives us accounts like that in Genesis 37 – 50 to build our confidence so we can trust him with our lives.

Death and deceit

Read Genesis 50:15-18

Jacob has died.

❓ *What do Joseph's brothers fear will happen now, and what do they do?*

Joseph has done a lot of weeping! I think there are two reasons he cries here: first, I suspect he knows Jacob said nothing of the sort, and he realises that his brothers still don't fully trust him. Second, this is the first time that they have explicitly confessed their sin against Joseph to Joseph.

Note that having sold Joseph into slavery at the start of the story, they now offer themselves as slaves at the end.

Narrative > analogy

Read Genesis 50:19-21

❓ *What does Joseph teach about God's providence—his sovereign control over people and events?*

❓ *Why does this understanding enable him not to seek vengeance against them?*

Three key truths, or three strands, weave together to form God's tapestry of history:

1. God is unstoppably powerful to do whatever pleases him.
2. God uses that power for our good—what pleases him is to bless his people.
3. We are responsible for what we do.

Can you think of an analogy for this? It's a bit like… Actually, it's not like anything else! It's not like an author writing a story, or a parent who knows what their child will do, or a programmer with a robot, or a chessmaster anticipating an opponent's moves.

That's why, instead of giving us an explanation, God gives us a narrative, so we can see how this works out in reality. The most important thing is not that we can explain it but that we learn to trust him.

The central event of all history fits this pattern. **Read Acts 2:23.** It is often mysterious, and it is always wonderful, and it is a rock to stand on when life is hard.

☑ Apply

❓ *Which of the three strands do you most struggle to believe? Why is clinging on to it good news when you face trials?*

⌃ Pray

Ask the Holy Spirit to drill the sovereignty and goodness of God deep into your heart so you would trust him, however dark life gets and however long the darkness lasts.

There is always hope

Whether it's in sport, or movies and stories, or politics, everyone loves a comeback— where we thought it was all over… and then it wasn't.

Two happy endings

Read Genesis 50:22-26

❷ *What do we learn about the end of Joseph's life from verses 22-23?*

It's a picture of fulfilment—full of years and full of family. After all the struggle and hardship, God has granted Joseph a happy ending.

❷ *Who does Joseph give instructions to about his death?*

It's no longer a family; it's now a nation!

❷ *What does he ask them to do?*

Joseph knows that the contented years in Egypt are not the ultimate happy ending. There is something more to come.

When hope dies

Think back through Genesis 37 – 50.

❷ *At which moments might Joseph have justifiably felt that hope had died and that it was all over for him?*

But in time he would learn that the story was not over; hope was not dead. Even now, as he prepares to die, he has hope for the future.

Centuries later, it will look as if hope really has died. Can you imagine anything more hopeless than the situation faced by Jesus' family and followers on the night he died?

As his disciples put it, on the road to Emmaus, "We *had* hoped..." (Luke 24:21). What hope could there be now that Jesus had died? But, again, the story was not yet over...

✔ Apply

We must learn not to judge things until the story is complete. Too often we look at the circumstances of our lives and think that God has forgotten us or that everything is beyond hope. The long, slow story of Joseph teaches us to trust and wait in the darkness.

❷ *Can you think of times when you had given up hope in a situation only for things to turn around?*
❷ *Are there areas of your life where you have effectively given up hope of change?*

When can we expect everything to work out? **Read Psalm 16:9-11**. It truly isn't all over. Hold on till Jesus returns!

⌃ Pray

Pray that God would breathe hope into you through these chapters, so that you would pray and live with a trust in God no matter what happens, as you look forward to eternal life.

Our plans, God's future

When things don't seem to be working out... when friends or family do mad things... when there's a sudden change in circumstances that leaves you feeling rattled...

When an exciting but scary opportunity comes up... when the world seems to be going crazy around you...

> ❷ *What is the most reassuring thing about the Christian faith?*

Read Proverbs 16:1-9, 33

His plan

> ❷ *What does each verse teach us about God?*
> ❷ *How would you summarise the whole?*

The absolute sovereignty and control of God is what lies behind all these sayings. They are supposed to fill us with a great confidence in the outcome of things—because ultimate control is in his wise and safe hands.

Our plans

Thinking about these things can cause confusion: *if God is in charge, what's the point in making my own decisions and choices?* But that's not what these truths are supposed to do. The Bible also teaches the opposite (complementary) truth: that we are free to make choices and that we are responsible for them. See how these Proverbs paint the full picture:

> ❷ *What should we bear in mind when we make plans (v 1)?*
> ❷ *Why is it important for us to realise the truth of verse 2?*

> ❷ *Is verse 3 a blanket promise, do you think? If not, what does it encourage us to do practically?*
> ❷ *Why are verses 4 and 5 so important for us to understand?*
> ❷ *What else is central to God's plan (v 6)?*
> ❷ *What does verse 33 encourage us to believe about seemingly "random" events? (Note: casting lots = rolling dice.)*

☑ Apply

> ❷ *What advice would you give from verse 9 to a Christian who is struggling to know how to be guided over a significant life event?*

� Pray

What plans are you working on at the moment—at work, in your family, at church? There are some things to pray through in the light of these verses:

- Ask God to reveal your true motives (v 2) and to help you seek his glory.

- Commit to godliness in the way you are achieving this plan (v 8).

- Dedicate your future to the Lord and to giving to him all the praise and glory for any plans that come to fruition.

- Pray verse 3.

Bible in a year: 2 Samuel 23-24 • Colossians 1

Lessons from Genesis

"It is not the end; it is not even the beginning of the end, but it is, perhaps, the end of the beginning." Churchill was not writing about Genesis 50, but he could have been.

Read Genesis 3:15

God's promise to defeat the serpent/snake—the devil—drives the narrative of Genesis. It is the story of a war—the great battle between God and evil, with the fate of humanity dependent on the outcome.

The poison

❓ *Sometimes the serpent attacks God's people directly. Where have we seen this in Genesis 32 – 50?*

We've also seen that the serpent's poison is not only a problem "out there"; it's also "in here". If anything, the greatest danger to God's people in Genesis is themselves.

❓ *How have you seen this through chapters 32 – 50?*

The promise

In Genesis 3:15 God promised that a child born to a woman would crush the serpent and undo the curse of sin and death. The rest of the Bible is the story of how he did that. As we trace the development of that promise through the second half of Genesis, we learn three key lessons about God:

1. God works through sinners

❓ *Be honest—which character have you found most obnoxious?!*

Isn't it amazing that God uses people like that! Foolish, lustful, weak, proud, violent,

unkind. God is the only hero—so there's no need to airbrush out the sins of Jacob and co. And if God can use people like that, he can use you too—so get on with serving him!

2. God works slowly: We end Genesis still centuries away from the coming of Jesus. Genesis teaches us to be patient and to trust God's timing: **read 2 Peter 3:8-9**.

❓ *As you look back over Genesis 32 – 50, when would you have struggled to trust God most if you had been there?*

3. God works unstoppably: Like a glacier, God is unstoppable. Think of all the challenges God faces—and overcomes—to keep working out his plans. Childless couples, warring families, hostile armies, sinful hearts, slavery, prison. Nothing can keep God from fulfilling his promise. In the light of all that, enjoying **reading Romans 8:37-39.**

⌄ Apply

Christ has won (Colossians 2:15), but we are still in a battle. **Read Ephesians 6:10-18.**

❓ *How do you need to stand firm today?*
❓ *How do the promises of God enable you to do so?*
❓ *If you had to sum up in a sentence what the Spirit has shown you about God, and yourself, through Genesis 32 – 50, what would you say?*

Use your answer to prompt your praise and prayers.

JOHN: A true testimony

*We rejoin John at the moment when the crucified Jesus has just bowed his head and given up his spirit. John wants us to be clear **that** he died—and **why** he died.*

Read John 19:31-35

Breaking the legs would make it impossible for the crucified person to raise themselves up on their legs to gasp another tortured breath: they would quickly suffocate. The Jewish leaders want to "finish off" the Son of God before it comes to the Sabbath.

❓ *Why don't the soldiers break Jesus' legs?*
❓ *Why do you think they decide to pierce his side?*

But why does such a careful author include what seems like a lot of extraneous detail?

Blood and water

Part of the answer may be medical. Modern doctors have confirmed that such a flow of "blood and water" would be taken today as a certain sign that the patient is definitively dead. The soldiers, who had surely pierced many people before, recognised that Jesus was dead. This, of course, is important because the miracle of the resurrection of Jesus from the dead is only a miracle if Jesus was truly dead in the first place.

❓ *What else does John say in verse 35 to help us believe?*

Scripture fulfilled

Read John 19:36-37

John gives another reason for why he records these details: they happened so that

Scripture would be fulfilled. The piercing of Jesus and the fact that his bones were not broken were not accidental, but rather all part of God's deliberate plan.

···· **TIME OUT** ····

John's first quotation is from Psalm 34:20. It also refers to the Passover lamb, whose bones were not to be broken (Exodus 12:46).

Read Exodus 12:21-27. The Passover lamb represented God's rescue of the Israelites from slavery and death. Jesus is the fulfilment of this sacrifice—finally liberating his people from sin and death.

The second quote is from Zechariah 12:10, where God promises to pour out a spirit of grace and supplication, while his people mourn for the one whom they have pierced.

❓ *Where in these passages is there something to celebrate?*
❓ *Where is there a sense of pain or grief?*
❓ *What reasons are there for us, too, to feel both joy and grief when we think of the cross?*

🔼 Pray

Consider what it means for you that Jesus died, and spend time in worship.

Pray for those you know who do not believe. Ask for opportunities to share with them the truth of John's testimony and the difference it has made to you.

Secret disciples

Jesus is dead and his body has been taken down from the cross. It is at this moment that his secret disciples finally fulfil their commitment to Christ.

The body of Jesus

The King is dead. All is finished. But the true sense of Jesus' words, "It is finished," is known only in the counsels of heaven at this point.

> ❷ *If you had been one of Jesus' followers, what would you have been thinking, feeling and doing at this point?*

Read John 19:38-42

Joseph of Arimathea was a rich man (Matthew 27:57) and a member of the Jewish ruling council (Mark 15:43) who had not consented to the decision of the council to kill Jesus (Luke 23:51). But he was a *secret* disciple (John 19:38).

Nicodemus was also a member of the ruling council (3:1). He is never explicitly said by John to be a follower of Jesus, but the suggestion is that he was moving in that direction. First he came to Jesus secretly at night (3:1-15); then he objected to the decision of the chief priests to condemn Jesus (7:51).

> ❷ *Does it surprise you that these are the men who take charge of Jesus' burial?*
> ❷ *Why do you think they do so?*

Let us not be too quick to judge a new follower of Jesus if they are not yet able to overcome their fear of going public with their faith. That said, discipleship should in the end express itself in some way, as it does with Joseph and Nicodemus here.

These disciples have not yet seen Jesus resurrected. Yet they fulfil their commitment to him by honouring him in death.

Burial customs

> ❷ *How do the men treat Jesus' body (19:39-40)?*
> ❷ *Where do they lay it (v 41-42)?*

Joseph and Nicodemus do their part. They do all they can to follow God and his word, even in these details of following Jewish burial customs and avoiding working on the Sabbath. They strive to keep a clear conscience before God and are willing to stand up and bear a cost to do so. Compare this with the attitude of the religious leaders to the Sabbath and Passover, which they have desecrated with their murder of Christ, while trying to cover up that deed by wanting him to be put to death more speedily.

▾ Apply

> ❷ *When do you find it hardest to be open about your faith in Christ?*
> ❷ *What could you do to express your devotion to Christ and the gospel of the cross in some public way?*

The empty tomb

Darkness hangs over the land, for the Messiah is dead.
Or is he?

The stone removed
Read John 20:1-2

The Sabbath has passed, and it is now the first day of the week—what we call Sunday. It is so early that it is "still dark". John uses the literal to invoke the symbolic: things seemed dark to Mary Magdalene.

> ❷ *What do you think would have been going through Mary's head as she went to the tomb?*
> ❷ *What does she think has happened to Jesus' body?*
> ❷ *What do her words and actions show about her attitude to Jesus?*

Tombs were cut into rock and had large stones rolled over their entrances to keep animals and robbers away. It would take several strong men to be able to move such a stone.

Mary Magdalene is the first witness to the resurrection. The significance of this should not be lost. First, she was a woman. This shows that women have a credibility and honour that ran counter to the culture of first-century Judea, where they did not have the legal status to be eyewitnesses in a court of law. Second, she had a less than reputable background. According to Luke 8:2, seven demons had been cast out of her. Yet it was Mary whom God chose to be the first witness of the resurrection of Jesus.

The strips of linen
Read John 20:3-10

John describes the reactions of different personalities to these events, thereby giving real credibility to his account of the physical resurrection of Jesus. Peter arrives at the tomb second but goes straight in (v 6) while the other disciple (probably John himself) hangs back.

> ❷ *What do you think the disciples were expecting to see in the tomb?*
> ❷ *Why is it important to note that the grave clothes are still there?*

John explains in verse 9 that the disciples did not expect Jesus to rise from the dead. Later they would realise that the Scriptures as a whole only make sense when we see that they have been fulfilled in the resurrection of the Christ. But as yet they did not understand this key to unlocking the mysteries of the Scriptures—John (the other disciple) was persuaded purely on the basis of what his eyes saw.

☑ Apply

> ❷ *What reasons are there in this passage to believe in Jesus' resurrection?*
> ❷ *Why does it matter that Jesus really, physically rose from the dead?*

Mary's message

Having rooted the story in fact, John now shows us the feeling that the events produced. We join Mary, alone at the tomb, weeping…

Why are you crying?
Read John 20:11-16

The one Mary has so loved is dead, and she has no idea what is now going on. Where is the body? Is there some extra cruelty still to come?

❷ *What is the surprise in verse 12?*

The angels are in white, indicating the purity and holiness not just of themselves but of the One they are serving. They are seated, indicating the victory that has been won by Christ. One is at the head and one at the foot—emphasising the empty space between them. But Mary does not understand. You can hear the emotion behind her anguished answer to the angels' question in verse 13.

❷ *What is the surprise in verse 14?*

Why does Mary not recognise Jesus? Perhaps because it is too good to be true: Mary knows that Jesus has died and does not expect to see him alive. What is more, there is something different, new, greater about the resurrection body of Jesus. We see the same lack of recognition in 21:4 and Luke 24:13-16.

❷ *What is the surprise in John 20:16?*

When the sight of Jesus fails to trigger faith in Mary, the word of Jesus brings her to her senses. "Rabboni," she exclaims—the affectionate form of "Rabbi".

Pray

Lord, help me to love you as Mary does, even when I don't fully understand you. Help me to know you and recognise your work in my life. Amen.

I have seen the Lord!
Read John 20:17-18

Mary acts appropriately in adoring Jesus, but he tells her not to hold onto him. The attitude that Jesus is encouraging is one not of passive amazement but of active mission. She is not to cling onto him but to share him.

❷ *What task does Jesus give Mary?*
❷ *What does Jesus say he is going to do next?*

The work of Jesus on the cross has now opened up the throne room of heaven so that Jesus' disciples can have an intimate relationship with the Father God through faith in the Son of God. He is now their Father as well as the Son's Father!

Apply

❷ *Do you think Mary found it easy to stop holding onto Jesus and go to share the news?*
❷ *Are you ever tempted towards passive amazement only? What does active mission look like for you?*

The locked room

Peace, joy and power in mission: Jesus' resurrection will transform his disciples.

Read John 20:19-20

❷ *How do the disciples feel at the beginning of the evening, and why?*

❷ *How does the tone change when Jesus arrives?*

Jesus does not say, *Why are you hiding in this room with the doors locked? Did you not know that I was going to rise again? How many times did I tell you?* No, his first words to his disciples are words of peace. Their response is joy; the Lord is risen, and death has been defeated!

······ TIME OUT ···

Jesus' resurrection body is fully physical, and yet it is also different. It is able to go through locked doors and suddenly come and stand among the disciples. This glorious reality awaits all those who trust in Christ. One day our bodies too will be raised imperishable.

Read 1 Corinthians 15:42-44

❷ *How does this passage describe Christ's body?*

❷ *How does it feel to know it will one day apply to you too?*

I am sending you

Read John 20:21-23

Jesus repeats to the disciples the truth that peace is now theirs. But here he adds a word of mission. This is so important. The presence of Jesus gives peace and joy, and the commission of Jesus compels us to share these by sharing him.

But this is not a task that is done by human brilliance, in our own strength or power. Jesus gives the disciples the Holy Spirit.

How is it that the Holy Spirit could be given here and also on the day of Pentecost (Acts 2:1-4)? The Spirit is given here as he was in the Old Testament—for times of special anointing and power (e.g. Exodus 31:3; Deuteronomy 34:9; Judges 3:10, 6:34; 1 Samuel 10:6). At Pentecost, the Spirit would be given in a new way, to all believers. So this giving of the Spirit in John 20 is a precursor of and preparation for Pentecost.

❷ *What does the gift of the Spirit mean that the disciples will do (John 20:22-23)?*

Jesus' commission to the disciples is to send them as the Father sent him (v 21). The forgiving of sins is connected to the proclamation of the gospel of Jesus Christ. If someone comes to believe in Christ, we can declare that their sins are forgiven.

◪ Pray

Ask God for peace and joy, both for yourself and for those you know.

Ask God to empower you to share Christ with those around you.

Bible in a year: Ezra 6-8 · 2 Timothy 3

The king's way

Proverbs was most likely compiled by Solomon and incorporates some specific sayings aimed at those who rule or lead in some way.

....

Read Proverbs 16:10-15

Solomon is writing about the duties and character of the king.

- ❓ *What characteristics should rulers cultivate in their lives?*
- ❓ *How might this apply to those with other responsibilities: in church, for example?*

Read Proverbs 16:16-32

The rest of the chapter contains a variety of proverbs on differing subjects. As you read them, pick out just three, and write the verse numbers below:

- ❓ *Find one that you think is especially appropriate to yourself.*
- ❓ *Find one that you think may be appropriate to someone you know.*

We'd be honoured if any members of the royal family or government ministers used *Explore* every day. But many of us have comparable (if lesser) responsibilities: parents, teachers, business people, leaders at youth groups or in the church.

- ❓ *Choose one verse that you think might apply to one of your areas of responsibility.*

⌃ Pray

Ask the Lord to help you live up to the challenges of these proverbs.

⌄ Apply

Growing in personal godliness is a matter of slow progress, often with relapses and failures. Here are some ways that you could start to imprint your chosen proverbs on your life:

- Write one out on a card and keep it with you as a reminder.
- Look through your diary and/or address book. Confess to God the times when you have not lived up to the standard set by the proverb regarding other people or things which you have done.
- Now pray for future events, meetings, and so on, that you would live by the truth of the verse.

Sharing these truths with others might be a little more difficult. What do you think about these ideas?

- Write a letter or a postcard to your friend, quoting the verse you picked out for them. You'll need to show love and humility.
- Commit yourself to living out the verse you chose for the person you know. Model the quality it praises for others to see.

⌃ Pray

Spend some time in prayer, asking God to bring the truth of these verses home to yourself and others, and to make you a humble and truthful encourager.

Thomas's doubts

But not all of the disciples have seen the risen Jesus. Enter Thomas, that famous doubter...

Prove it

Read John 20:24-25

> ❓ *Why doesn't Thomas believe that Jesus has risen?*

Thomas is only really asking for the same evidence that the other disciples have had. He is just dramatising his desire for evidence, for physical proof. Perhaps we should call him not "Doubting Thomas" but "Prove it Thomas".

My Lord and my God!

Read John 20:26-28

Thomas has to wait a week to see the evidence. Once again, the doors are locked, and, in a repeat performance, Jesus suddenly stands among them and declares peace to them. This time, Thomas is there.

> ❓ *How does Jesus express kindness towards Thomas?*
> ❓ *How does he rebuke him?*

Jesus tells Thomas to do exactly what he had insisted he would need to do in order to believe. But we have no record of Thomas actually putting his hands into Jesus' wounds. Seeing, for Thomas, is believing.

Then doubting Thomas becomes worshipping Thomas! Note the personal tone that he adopts: *my* Lord and *my* God. Here is adoration of Jesus as God in the setting of intimacy with Jesus as Brother.

⌃ Pray

Try addressing Jesus as "My Lord and my God" in your prayers.

> ❓ *What difference will it make that he is Lord and God?*
> ❓ *What difference will it make that he is your Lord and God?*

That you may believe

Read John 20:29-31

> ❓ *What does it mean to believe in Jesus?*

John picks up on Jesus' words, inviting those who have not seen him to believe. We are blessed if we believe on the basis of the eyewitness testimony recorded here. This is John's whole purpose in writing: to help us, like Thomas, to believe—and to have life, "life ... to the full" (10:10).

⌄ Apply

Jesus gives Thomas the evidence he demands. At the same time, he tells him that he needs to actually believe. In order to sit on a chair, you need to believe that it can hold your weight—and real belief will mean actually sitting down on it. Thomas is being told to "sit down"—to actually trust Jesus.

> ❓ *Is there any evidence you need to ask God for, to help you believe?*
> ❓ *What would it look like for you, today, to simply put your trust in Jesus?*

 Bible in a year: 1 Chronicles 1-3 • Jude

Best breakfast ever

The disciples seem to be going back to normal life. But Jesus isn't finished with them, and so normal will never be the same again.

Read John 21:1-6

Jesus comes and stands on the shore, but no one recognises him. He calls out to them: "Friends," he shouts across—literally, "Children". It is an affectionate term of endearment.

> ❷ *What does Jesus say next?*
> ❷ *Why doesn't he just tell the disciples who he is, do you think?*

It is instructive that the disciples in the Gospels never catch any fish unless Jesus is with them!

Jesus reveals who he is by miraculously bringing into their net an extraordinarily large catch.

It is the Lord!

Read John 21:7-14

> ❷ *How do each of the disciples respond to what has happened?*
> ❷ *What do they find when they reach the shore?*

Jesus doesn't say, *Why did you not recognise me?* or *What are you doing back in Galilee?* or *I have work for you to do.* No: "Come and have breakfast".

Next their Lord takes bread and gives it to them, and does the same with the fish. He gives out the food as they sit down together around the fire, next to the lake, in this early morning. What a picture of peace and joy!

☑ Apply

Jesus disciples people by making time to be with them—over meals, in person, in the flow of life. Our churches, likewise, are to be places of relationship, love and fellowship with Christ and with each other.

> ❷ *Do you ensure that you take time to sit and have fellowship with Jesus?*
> ❷ *What Christian brother or sister could you make time to sit down with this week?*

☒ Pray

Jesus meets the disciples in their home territory as they go about ordinary tasks.

> ❷ *Is there any ordinary part of your life where you struggle to see or to serve God?*

Lift that to the Lord and ask him to be with you in all you do.

Three appearances

John tells us in verse 14 that this was now the third time Jesus had appeared to the disciples. Each appearance communicated something specific about his resurrection. The first was to give the disciples peace, joy and the Holy Spirit. The second was to give Thomas faith. This third is for fellowship—and, as we will see in the next study, for restoration.

Bible in a year: 1 Chronicles 4-6 • Luke 1 v 1-20

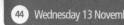
Life after failure

There is an elephant in the room—Peter's failure to acknowledge Jesus outside the courtroom when Jesus was on trial.

❷ *Are there any ways in which you feel you have failed Jesus recently?*

❷ *Are there others you know who have failed and fallen away?*

Do you love me?

Read John 21:15-17

As John brings his Gospel to a close, he shows us the reinstatement of Peter. Clearly "life ... to the full" (10:10) is on offer for all who believe (20:31)—including for those who fail. Peter is acknowledged by Jesus as his follower and his under-shepherd.

···· TIME OUT ·······························

Read John 18:15-18, 25-27 to remind yourself of Peter's denials.

·······························

Jesus calls Peter "Simon son of John". The last time he used this name was back in John 1, before he gave him a new name to indicate his calling: Peter, the "rock" (1:42). Now he calls him by his original name. It must have been obvious to Peter that Jesus was bringing him back to his first calling.

❷ *What questions does Jesus ask Peter in 21:15-17?*

❷ *What commands does he give him?*

More than these

Peter had previously seemed to place himself ahead of the other disciples by claiming that he would lay down his life for Jesus (13:37). But now he has been taught by the bitter experience of failure to be humbler. He does not reply that he loves Jesus more than the other disciples do—merely that he loves Jesus (21:15). Peter is not superior to the other disciples. All of them love Jesus.

You know I love you

❷ *Why does Peter feel hurt by Jesus' third question?*

Jesus is seeking to raise in Peter's mind the memory of his thrice-repeated denial. It is good for Peter to hear himself say three times over "I love you" when once he had said three times over "I don't know him".

⌃ Pray

Reflect on how much you love Jesus, and how you may have failed to show that love.

Ask God for mercy for your failings. Know that in Christ you are forgiven and restored. Ask for his help in following him once again.

Pray for others who have failed. Ask for forgiveness for them, and for the love of Jesus to be in them, so they can serve God and minister to others.

Ask for wisdom to know how to shepherd those who feel wounded by their failures.

 Bible in a year: 1 Chronicles 7-9 • Luke 1 v 21-38

Feeding and following

"You know that I love you!" Peter has said. Now Jesus reminds him of what it means to love to the end.

Feed my sheep

Read John 21:15-17

> ❷ *What did we learn about Peter's attitude towards Jesus?*
> ❷ *How do Jesus' commands show his attitude towards Peter?*

Jesus has called Peter to be his under-shepherd, feeding the flock with God's word and taking care of them.

Read John 21:18-19

> ❷ *What else is in store for Peter?*

Jesus explained in 10:11 that being a good shepherd means laying down one's life for the sheep. This is love in action; this is what Jesus himself did.

Jesus' prophecy of Peter's death is specific. In being told that he will "stretch out [his] hands", Peter is being told that he will die on a cross.

···· **TIME OUT** ·······························

Read John 17:1-4

Jesus' death glorifies God because it brings people into eternal life and the knowledge of God. It also shows Jesus' total obedience to his Father, which itself brings them both glory.

> ❷ *In what ways will Peter's death be different to that of Jesus?*
> ❷ *In what ways will it be similar?*

> ❷ *Why do you think John tells us that Peter's death will glorify God (21:19)?*

What about him?

Read John 21:20-23

Peter turns and sees John ("the disciple whom Jesus loved") following them. If this is how Peter is going to die, he wants to know what will happen to John.

> ❷ *How does Jesus respond?*

⌄ Apply

We cannot know what God's plans are for every individual—not even for ourselves. Our responsibility is simply to love Jesus and to follow him (v 22). If that means that we are called literally to give up our lives for him, then we must be willing to.

> ❷ *How can you follow Peter's example to "take care of" and "feed" other believers you know?*
> ❷ *What costs do you think following Jesus in this way could have?*

⌃ Pray

Lord Jesus, you died to bring eternal life to those who love you. Help me to love you more. Help me to love those who love you. Build my faith so that I may be willing to lay down anything and everything for you. Use my life to bring glory to the Father. Amen.

Closing statement

John finishes his Gospel by revealing his own identity—and reminding us once again of all that Jesus has done.

Read John 21:24-25

This is the disciple

John tells us that the man he has been calling "the disciple whom Jesus loved" (v 20) is in fact himself. He is the one who wrote this Gospel.

The phrase is first used during the Last Supper (13:23). After that, it is used several times during chapters 19 – 21.

Read John 19:26-27 and 20:1-10

> ❷ *How would you describe John?*
> ❷ *How does he present himself?*

He testifies

21:25 tells us that when we read John's Gospel, we are not reading all that took place, but we are reading all that we need to know. John has carefully selected his material to communicate the message of Jesus.

Read John 19:33-35 and 21:6-7

In these passages John speaks specifically about what "the disciple whom Jesus loved" saw and said.

> ❷ *What are some key things that John testifies to?*

His testimony is true

When John says, "We know that his testimony is true" (v 24) he is talking of the apostolic "we"—the authority of the apostles, who were commissioned by Christ (16:13). He says something very similar in 1 John 4:6 about his authority and that of the other apostles to write Scripture and speak for Christ: "We are from God, and whoever knows God listens to us; but whoever is not from God does not listen to us. This is how we recognise the Spirit of truth and the spirit of falsehood."

This Gospel was written by an apostle of Christ, and the apostles of Christ say it is true. Therefore, our part is to read, listen, believe and obey.

> ❷ *What do you think John wants you to think and feel as you finish his Gospel?*

Apply

Look back over all that Jesus has done and said in John 19 – 21; or, if you have time, glance through the whole of John's Gospel.

> ❷ *What struck you as surprising?*
> ❷ *What did you find most moving?*
> ❷ *What response should you make?*

Pray

Reflect on how God's Spirit has been prompting you to love God's Son more deeply and serve him more committedly, through the words of the disciple John. Ask God for help in living out this change.

2 TIMOTHY: Dear son

Timothy was not Paul's physical son, but the relationship between the two men was as deep and profound as if they had been related.

Who's who?
Read 2 Timothy 1:1-5

❓ *How does Paul describe Timothy in verse 2? (See also 1 Timothy 1:2.)*

❓ *What do we learn about Timothy's biological family in 2 Timothy 1:5?*

Paul remembers Timothy constantly in his prayers (v 3). He longs to see him again and recalls Timothy's tears (presumably over their separation). Such a reunion would fill Paul with joy (v 4). This special relationship between Paul and Timothy is reflected in the other references to Timothy in Paul's letters (for example, Philippians 2:19-22).

Timothy's sincere faith did not commence with him but with his grandmother first and then also with his mother (2 Timothy 1:5). We do not hear of his father. In Acts 16:1-3 we are told that his mother, and presumably his grandmother also, were Jewish, but that his father was Greek. Paul is persuaded that the faith of Timothy's mother and grandmother "lives in you also" (2 Timothy 1:5).

⌄ Apply

❓ *Are you a parent or grandparent? An uncle or aunt? Or are there children or younger adults you influence, even if you are not biologically related?*

❓ *How will you teach them the Scriptures so they may share your faith in Jesus?*

Fan into flame
Read 2 Timothy 1:6-8

❓ *What do we learn about Timothy's gift?*

❓ *How will the Spirit work in him (v 7)?*

When Paul reminds Timothy to "fan into flame the gift of God" (v 6), it does not necessarily mean that the flame was flickering or dying. Timothy is about to be charged with an extraordinary task that needs all the supernatural strength that comes from God. The nature of Timothy's gift is not explained. However, in the parallel passage in 1 Timothy 4:13-14 the gift concerns the ministry of the word. This view ties in with 2 Timothy 1:7-8, where "the Spirit [of] power, love and self-discipline" are needed for "the testimony about our Lord".

"Power" is the ability to get things done. The particular power that we Christians have is the power to endure our cross. "Love" is necessary, as it is critical in this ministry to think of others rather than self. To lay down your life for others and their salvation is the essence of love. And "self-control" is needed if we are to live not by our passions and emotions but by the wisdom of knowing what is right and doing it.

⌃ Pray

Pray that the Spirit will give you "power, love and self-discipline" to enable you to share gospel truth this week.

How should we live?

Proverbs not only helps us to see the best way to go but warns us about the bad. These verses encapsulate the failure of life without God, of logic without the Lord.

Read Proverbs 16:25, 30

> ❷ *What mistakes do the people in these verses make?*
> ❷ *What results from them?*

People the world over make choices about how to live, what to do, where to spend their money, what to invest time in. Most do things because they have good reason to—often with good evidence. But life without the wisdom from above will only ever lead to death.

The person in verse 25 is just doing what they think is right, but the person in verse 30 is ruled by deviousness. He or she is using the nod and the wink to convey secret messages as they hatch a dishonest plan. So how do you make your decisions? Not just the big ones about which job, which partner, which church, and so on—but the smaller ones that make up the sum of our daily lives: how you spend your money and time; what you read; what you talk about; what you watch or listen to. Unless the knowledge of God—the fear of the LORD—is influencing these decisions, then we will be Christian in name only.

Not like this
Read Proverbs 16:27-29

> ❷ *What impact do the words of these four characters have?*

✔ Apply

Although these verses express something that is obviously evil, the application may be closer to home than we realise.

> ❷ *Think of the way you talk about others in church or at work. Now read verse 28 again and ask, "Am I guilty of this kind of talk?"*

Notice that the focus is not on whether what we say is true—that is our standard excuse for gossiping in this way—but on the effect it has on others.

> ❷ *Is there something you need to repent of or pray about?*

But like this
Read Proverbs 16:32

Warriors and "city-takers" were the great heroes of the day.

> ❷ *So what is this verse saying (think about the types of people who are held up as heroes in our culture today)?*

The issue is not how much we have achieved or what position we have attained but what our character is. Have we taken control of our sinful hearts and bent them to God's glory, or are we allowing spite and pride to rule our words and actions?

> ❷ *How does your answer encourage or challenge you?*

Bible in a year: 1 Chronicles 19-21 • Luke 2 v 25-52

Not ashamed

Before reading today's passage, ask yourself when and why you might be tempted to be ashamed of your faith or of other Christians.

2 Timothy is Paul's letter requesting Timothy to visit him and bring supplies: his friend Mark, his cloak, his books and parchments (4:11-13). But potentially the request involved both fear and shame for Timothy...

Read 2 Timothy 1:8-18

❷ *What does Paul tell Timothy to do, and not to do, in verse 8?*

❷ *How would verses 9-14 encourage Timothy as he aims to obey verse 8?*

Timothy was to share in suffering for the gospel, and was to do so by the power of God. This suffering for the gospel by the power of God is spelt out in the subsequent verses. Timothy was not working to his own plan but to God's (v 9).

Paul describes himself as the Lord's prisoner (v 8). Both the Romans and the Jews may have thought that Paul was their prisoner. But Paul knew he was in prison because of Jesus, the sovereign Ruler over the world. So Timothy, whose faith was in Christ Jesus our Lord, was not to be ashamed of Paul, Jesus' prisoner.

⌃ Pray

When are you tempted to be ashamed of the gospel or of its messengers? Ask the Lord to give you courage, through his Spirit, to stand firm for the gospel this week.

❷ *What do we learn about shame in verses 8, 12 and 16?*

At the time of writing, Paul may look to be beaten, his Saviour may look weak and his gospel may look wrong. But Paul is not ashamed of his Lord or of testifying to him, for he knows and is persuaded of the truth of the gospel, and so he keeps his faith firmly in God.

Paul is also encouraged that Onesiphorus is not ashamed of him (v 16). It is so easy to be ashamed of the gospel, of gospel preachers, and even of the Lord of the gospel. Yet Jesus warned us not to be ashamed of him (Mark 8:38); and, thankfully, he was not ashamed but "endured the cross, scorning its shame", thus setting an example that Timothy—and we—must follow (Hebrews 12:1-2).

⌄ Apply

"I know whom I have believed, and am convinced that he is able to guard what I have entrusted to him until that day."
(2 Timothy 1:12)

❷ *When are you tempted to lose confidence that God will guard what you have entrusted to him?*

"What you heard from me, keep as the pattern of sound teaching, with faith and love in Christ Jesus." (v 13)

❷ *How could you keep this pattern first in your own life, and then in teaching and modelling it to others?*

Not chained

In 2 Timothy 2:1, Paul again calls Timothy his "son"—and then goes on to unpack what "suffering for the gospel, by the power of God" (1:8) will actually look like.

Read 2 Timothy 2:1-7

❓ *Why does Timothy need to find "reliable people" (v 2)?*

❓ *What three illustrations of ministry does Paul use in verses 3-6?*

Paul's and Timothy's ministries were not to terminate with them in the first generation of Christians; for they paved the way for the gospel message to be preserved and transmitted to future generations. Here are four generations of gospel ministers. Paul and Timothy belong to the first two, and then the faithful men who teach others make up generations three and four. Here is the plan for the future—not establishing an institution but faithfully transmitting a message.

With three quickly stated illustrations, Paul outlines the internal discipline of the soldier, the athlete and the farmer. Each has to put their own pleasure and comfort aside as they undertake their task faithfully. The soldier must avoid civilian distractions, the athlete illegal shortcuts and the farmer laziness.

Remember, remember

Read 2 Timothy 2:8-13

❓ *What does Paul tell Timothy to remember in verse 8?*

❓ *Paul describes this as his "gospel". Why do you think these things would be important for the gospel message?*

In the area of sharing in suffering (1:8), it is especially critical to understand life in the light of Jesus "raised from the dead" (2:8). It is by his resurrection appearing that Jesus has abolished death and brought life and immortality to light. His conquest over sin and death and all the forces of evil is a great comfort to those who are now enduring suffering in his name.

Jesus was "descended from David"—the messianic king through whom God had promised to save his people and establish an eternal, universal kingdom. Indeed, this lay at the heart of Paul's gospel, for he preached that "the Messiah had to suffer and rise from the dead [saying] 'This Jesus I am proclaiming to you is the Messiah'" (Acts 17:3).

⌄ Apply

Paul is in prison, and yet he writes that "God's word is not chained" (2 Timothy 2:9).

❓ *In what situations this week will you need to remember that God's word can't be stopped?*

⌃ Pray

Re-read verses 11-13 and then turn each phrase into a prayer of thanks and praise.

The word of truth

In these next verses, Paul addresses Timothy as one who must "correctly handle the word of truth"—and also us as those who must live in the light of that truth.

Read 2 Timothy 2:14-26

Teaching the truth

❷ *What is Timothy to "remind" and "warn" people about (v 14)?*

❷ *What is he to do in verses 15-16?*

Words are important to any messenger or teacher. Messages are conveyed in words. Words are even more important for Christian teachers, as they are responsible for teaching the word of God (1 Peter 4:11; 1 Thessalonians 2:13); and the word of God is his creative power for salvation (Psalm 33:6; Romans 1:16-17; 1 Corinthians 1:18).

Yet, instead of listening to God's word, sinful people are quite capable of quarrelling and fighting over words (2 Timothy 2:14). Truth is contained and expressed in words, but people who are opposed or indifferent to the truth will dispute and argue about the words in which truth is expressed. It is a more civilised and yet still-arrogant form of "I don't like the message, so I will shoot the messenger"—but rather than shooting messengers, we kill the message by arguing about its wording.

⌃ Pray

Pray for those who teach the truth in your church: not just preachers but those who teach the children, lead small groups, do one-to-one Bible reading and so on.

2 Timothy 2:15 is a great statement of the work of all Christian ministry, from teaching our children at home to preaching to thousands in a stadium, and all stops between these. "Do your best" could also be translated "make every effort" or "pursue with zeal and fervour". It is not something to be lackadaisical about—just the reverse: it is to be done with enthusiasm and passion.

⌄ Apply

Whenever we teach, a Christian should always be one who "correctly handles the word of truth" (v 15).

❷ *Think through all the ways you will engage with the Bible this week— reading, listening, discussing, teaching... How can you be sure to handle and respond to God's word well?*

Living by the truth

Timothy was a young man, so Paul warns him about "the evil desires of youth" (v 22). But whatever our age or gender, there's plenty in Paul's list to challenge us all.

❷ *What particularly strikes you in verses 22-26?*

The way Timothy speaks about the truth must be correct (v 15) and godly (v 16) but also gentle (v 25).

❷ *How will you get that balance right?*

The last days

There is a time for everything under heaven, but it is very important to understand the times that we live in. This is the appeal of 2 Timothy 3:1-9.

❓ *What do you think of when you hear the phrase "the last days"?*

Read 2 Timothy 3:1-9

But mark this…

The last days (between Jesus' ascension and return) will be difficult because sinful people will still be sinful, and opposition to God and his people will grow. So, as the gospel is preached, we're to expect opposition, hostility, false teachers, false rumours and ridicule. And where opposition has institutional power, such as in government or ecclesiastical organisations, we are to expect persecution, discrimination and hostility.

It is easy to see this in the 21st century. We only have to look at the newspapers, watch the TV news, listen to the radio news broadcasts or watch people argue on the internet.

❓ *What might "a form of godliness" (v 5) look like, do you think?*

There is nothing wrong with having the appearance of godliness. All who are genuinely religious will have some form of godliness, of being religious and pious. The real problem with these people is that though they have the appearance of godliness, they at the same time deny its power. Here are people who oppose the truth of the gospel while practising the externals of Christianity! They do not believe what the gospel teaches but they are involved in what the Christian community does.

Denying the truth

These false teachers not only deny the truth; in denying it, they also deny the power of religion (v 5). This is the power of God found in the gospel: his power to save by the death and resurrection of Jesus; his power to transform lives now through the Spirit of the risen Lord Jesus; the power for us to endure suffering in this world because we know the saving power of Jesus.

It's easy to think we're not at risk from the false teachers Paul is warning against here…

❓ *But how does he describe the way they work (v 6)?*

Paul is adamant about what Timothy should do: "Have nothing to do with such people" (v 5). Not just avoid their *teaching* or their *ungodliness*, but avoid *such people themselves*. We are not to fellowship with those who maintain the form and appearance of godliness while denying its truth and power—for their false teaching and ways not only upset the faith of some but also spread like gangrene, killing and putrefying all who come into contact with them (see 1 Corinthians 5:9-13).

⌄ Apply

❓ *Are there those in your circles who look religious but do not teach the gospel? What would it look like for you to "have nothing to do with such people"?*

 Bible in a year: 2 Chronicles 1-3 • Luke 5 v 1-16

Stand firm

Paul has been telling Timothy what life will be like as a Christian between Jesus' ascension and return ("the last days", 3:1). It will involve suffering as Paul did...

Read 2 Timothy 3:10-13

❷ *What, if anything, would stop you from wanting to live a godly life?*

❷ *What will happen to "everyone who wants to live a godly life" (v 12)?*

At the time of writing, Paul was in prison, apparently facing death. And in all this suffering and persecution, he was a model of patient endurance and steadfastness.

Remarkably, up to this time, Paul was repeatedly rescued. He writes of "the persecutions I endured. Yet the Lord rescued me from all of them" (v 11). In the evil, difficult last days, the false prophets and teachers will make some progress; they will persuade and mislead people. But in the long run they will all fail (v 9). Yet Paul and the truth of the gospel did not fail. The Lord rescued him, and his message has transformed the rest of history, down to the present day.

When persecuted, reviled, dismissed, ridiculed or attacked, even physically, Christianity and Christians always look weak and defeated, while the enemies of the truth seem powerful and in control. But, in fact, God is always in control. So, not only will the enemies fail but God is able to rescue his servants from any or all of these attacks.

Godly or "goodly"?

The "godly life in Christ Jesus" (v 12) is code for the gospel and its proclamation for the salvation of mankind. The secret of godliness is the great confession of the gospel itself (1 Timothy 3:16). People are rarely persecuted for "goodliness". Being good and moral may goad the consciences of those around you but rarely to the point of persecution. But proclaiming and living the gospel of Jesus always creates a reaction. Those who do not know the truth are generally offended by the claim that "there is no other name under heaven given to mankind by which we must be saved" (Acts 4:12).

To live by and proclaim the name of Jesus in evil times will make you at least unpopular, if not outright persecuted. 2 Timothy 3:12 is not saying you will be persecuted every minute of every day, but that at some time or other you *will* be persecuted.

❷ *Have you ever been persecuted for your faith? Can you think of situations coming up where you will have the opportunity to stand up for the gospel?*

❷ *How will remembering Paul's words help you at that time?*

⌃ Pray

Which countries have been in the news this week because of wars or religious persecution? Pray for anyone you know who lives there, or individuals or mission agencies who serve there. If you don't know anyone specific to pray for, pray anyway! The Lord knows those who need your prayers.

But as for you…

In the light of all of Paul's ministry and persecutions, and the generality of persecutions, evil and imposters, Paul's command is simply "Continue"!

Read 2 Timothy 3:14-17

"Continue" sounds so pedestrian, so ordinary, so almost-boring. We could translate the Greek word as "remain" or "stay"—don't move. It hardly sounds exciting. Yet the true character of Christian faith is faithfulness.

However, what Timothy is to continue in is "what you have learned and have become convinced of" (v 14). The pressure of persecution and the seduction of deception must not see him move from what he has already learned and now firmly believes.

❷ *Who did Timothy learn from (v 14-15)?*

Timothy learned truth from his mother and grandmother (1:5) and also from Paul, whose life he followed carefully. He was able to do as Hebrews 13:7 commands: "Remember your leaders, who spoke the word of God to you. Consider the outcome of their way of life and imitate their faith."

☑ Apply

❷ *Who opens up the Bible for you?*
❷ *How can you "imitate their faith"?*

God-breathed

❷ *What is Scripture useful for and why (2 Timothy 3:15-17)?*

Without the gospel, the Old Testament Scriptures make you wise, and even prepare you for the coming of Jesus, but they do not, in themselves, teach you about salvation through faith in Jesus Christ. Yet with the coming of Jesus, the saving effect of the sacred writings has been greatly enhanced. For what was anticipated has now come, and what was prophesied has now been fulfilled. The Old Testament is not a dead letter, to be left behind now that the gospel of Jesus has arrived. The Old Testament is God's word, actively working in making Timothy wise for salvation through faith in Christ Jesus.

❷ *How well do you know the Old and New Testaments? What could you read or listen to, or who could you talk with, to get to know God's word better?*

The utility of Scripture is fourfold (v 16):

- *Teaching*—it shows us the truth and the right way to walk in life.
- *Rebuking*—it tells us when we go wrong and challenges our errors.
- *Correcting*—it explains how to get back on track and put things right again.
- *Training in righteousness*—it tells us and shows us the pathways of right living.

So the purpose and intent of the Scriptures is to finish and furnish "the servant of God". It is to complete or finish you in the righteous ways of life, furnished or equipped for every good work (v 17).

❷ *When you are preparing for a "good work" (v 17), do you start with the Bible? Why / why not?*

Where is God?

Remarkably, in these central chapters of Proverbs God is mentioned very little. But that doesn't mean he is absent...

Read Proverbs 17:1-15

- ❷ *Which verses explicitly mention God?*
- ❷ *What specific things do these verses teach about the character, purposes and activity of God in the world?*

Refining

Re-read Proverbs 17:3

- ❷ *What's the point of the word picture in the first half of the verse?*
- ❷ *How does that illuminate what the word "test" means in practice here?*

···· TIME OUT ····

The theme of God purifying our hearts, as gold and silver are purified by being melted them at extreme temperatures, is found throughout Scripture. Check out these verses if you have time: Psalm 66:10-12; Isaiah 48:9-11; Zechariah 13:8-9; Malachi 3:2-4; 1 Peter 1:7; 1 Corinthians 3:10-15.

⌄ Apply

- ❷ *Have you ever experienced God's work in this way in your heart?*
- ❷ *As you consider your walk with God, are there areas of your life where you need God's refining fire to do its work?*

Talk to the Lord about your answers.

Respect

Re-read Proverbs 17:5

- ❷ *What is the root problem with the attitudes in the two halves of verse 5?*
- ❷ *What will the result be if we leave these tendencies unchecked?*

Mockery is everywhere. But laughter is a dangerous response when we forget that God is both the Creator of all people and is in sovereign control of all things. When we allow our sense of humour to overcome our respect for God like this, we put ourselves in peril of judgment.

Rationalising

Re-read Proverbs 17:15

- ❷ *Why do you think God feels so strongly about these two things?*
- ❷ *When and how are you tempted to fall into either of these traps?*

God is the measure of both right and wrong. When we judge or defend a politician or a family member in a partisan way, we are playing God, which is why he finds such thinking abominable.

⌃ Pray

Ask the Lord to help you fine-tune your attitudes, so that you think and relate to the world and others in a way that pleases him.

How itchy are your ears?

"Ears that hear and eyes that see—the LORD has made them both" (Proverbs 20:12). How can you use your eyes and ears today to glorify the Lord?

Read 2 Timothy 4:1-5

The charge is given

❓ *In whose presence is Paul writing (v 1)?*
❓ *What difference does that make to his "charge" to Timothy?*

It is hard to think of a greater drumroll and fanfare than verse 1. But this is more than simply the sound of drums and brass to get us prepared. It is the important truth that God is witnessing the charge that Paul is declaring to Timothy—and not only God but also Christ Jesus.

Lest Timothy miss the significance of Jesus' presence, Paul reminds him that Jesus is going to judge the living and the dead. He is the one to whom Timothy is answerable, for we will all appear before the judgment seat of Christ—and he also now is in charge of the world as the risen King.

⌃ Pray

Those who preach in your church are also answerable to Christ. Pray that they will serve him faithfully, prepare diligently and teach patiently.

Preach the word

Timothy's task, which Paul lays upon him with such seriousness, is to proclaim the gospel. "Preach" does not mean stand in a pulpit but rather "proclaim" or "declare". The word of God is not a discussion-starter but a declaration. And Timothy's preaching (v 2) is to be *constant* (whether that is convenient or inconvenient), *confronting* (calling for repentance) and *continuous* (not a one-off activity).

Now Paul speaks of a time that will see hostility to the word of God. People will lose patience with sound teaching. This should not surprise us, given what is said of the "last days" (3:1).

✔ Apply

Choose your own teacher is widely practised in the globalised Christianity of the internet—as it was in Timothy's day (4:3).

❓ *How do you currently choose what teaching to listen to?*
❓ *How can you ensure that any online sermons you listen to contain "sound doctrine"?*

We are not all preachers. But we all have opportunities to use the Bible to "correct, rebuke and encourage—with great patience and careful instruction" (v 2).

❓ *Which of these (correct, rebuke or encourage) are you most likely to do? Do you need to change the balance between the three?*

In the departure lounge

As we near the end of 2 Timothy, we see Paul outlining the conclusion of his own life and ministry as the reason for Timothy to fan into flame the gift of God (2 Timothy 1:6).

Read 2 Timothy 4:6-8

Fought, finished, faith

❓ *What do we learn about Paul in these verses?*

❓ *And what about Jesus (see also v 1)?*

❓ *And what about ourselves?*

Paul metaphorically describes the certainty of his death by using the illustration of the outpouring of the drink offering. (This was an offering of water or wine that was poured on top of a sacrifice presented to God.) Paul is not saying his death will occur immediately but that the cup has been tipped and the drink is now pouring out. He then says the same thing more literally, though still in terms of "departure" rather than simply death. As a believer in the resurrection, Paul knows that death truly is only a departure.

That Paul is on the final lap, if not in the home straight, is clear from the three statements in the next verse: "I have fought the good fight, I have finished the race, I have kept the faith" (v 7). The fight is not a militaristic term, but more a gymnastic struggle. Paul does use militaristic language (for example, 1 Timothy 1:18), but here his choice of words is much more about the physical conflict of an athletic contest (as it is in 1 Corinthians 9:24-27). Therefore, it is easy to slip into the second statement of finishing a race. Yet both these images are really illustrating the key statement:

"I have kept the faith". Paul's point is not about fighting or running, though both require the effort and discipline that he commends to Timothy in 2 Timothy 2:4-6. The point he is making is that he has finished and finished well, for he has kept the faith.

⌄ Apply

❓ *How does thinking of death as a departure help when looking ahead to your own death?*

❓ *How does it add urgency when you think of loved ones who do not yet know Christ?*

Ready to depart

❓ *How do Paul's words about his "departure" (4:6) add gravity to his "charge" to Timothy (4:1)?*

The ESV translates the end of verse 8 as "all who have loved his appearing". Most commentators take "his appearing" to be Jesus' return on the judgment day. But his appearing is often his resurrection (1 Timothy 3:16; 2 Timothy 1:10). The perfect tense of the verb "to love" would reinforce the idea that on this occasion it is referring to Christians' love of his death and resurrection—which is the basis of every believer's salvation.

❓ *Do you love Jesus' death and resurrection (4:8)? What difference does that make to your daily life?*

Grace be with you

As we come to the end of Paul's letter, he has some practical matters to address, and some final, wonderful truths to share about God's sovereign control.

Read 2 Timothy 4:9-22

Real people

❷ *In these closing verses, Paul names 17 people. Which of them were helpful to Paul, and which did harm to him?*

❷ *Paul is writing from prison. What does verse 13 tell you about what that has been like for him (see also verse 21)?*

In some ways, we can feel that the letter finishes with something of an anticlimax after Paul's great statement of verses 6-8. He goes on to list all manner of administrative details that he wants Timothy to attend to. However, within this material there are some lessons for us to draw. Demas having left because "he loved this world" (v 10) is a very sad statement. Paul's need for a cloak before winter (v 13) shows that he was not an ascetic, denying himself basics such as warmth. His desire to keep reading and working is a great example to those who are tiring. His loving fellowship with others shows that his ministry was not a solo effort but one with many colleagues and protégés. And the list gives Christian names for future generations of believers' children!

⌄ Apply

❷ *Paul's enemies probably thought his arrest and imprisonment meant they had won, but how does Paul see things (v 16-18)?*

⌃ Pray

❷ *Can you think of any situations in your local area or country, or in the wider world, where it looks as if the enemies of Christianity are winning?*

Learn from Paul's confidence about the Lord's sovereign control to help yourself pray about those situations.

Final greetings

The final greeting (v 22) of Paul to Timothy wishes him personally the Lord's presence and, with all who read this letter, God's grace. So, as the letter commenced with a prayer for Timothy to receive grace from God, together with mercy and peace (1:2), it also finishes by wishing grace not only to him but to all who read it (for the last word, "you," is plural).

⌃ Pray

Look back through the whole of 2 Timothy.

❷ *What do you want to thank God for?*
❷ *What do you need to ask his help with?*
❷ *Who can you encourage with the truths God has been showing you?*

Turn all of these answers into prayer.

💧 *Bible in a year: 2 Chronicles 17-18 • Luke 8 v 1-25*

1 CORINTHIANS: Intro

Do you find that being a Christian puts you in conflict with the culture around you? So did the Corinthians....

Mission strategy

Corinth was a Roman colony situated on the narrow strip of land linking mainland Greece to the Peloponnesian peninsula. This meant that it drew a roaring trade from the sea traffic in both the eastern Mediterranean and the Aegean, and it was therefore quite a melting-pot of cultures and religions. The city boasted temples to numerous pagan gods, including Aphrodite, Hera and Apollo, as well as a Jewish synagogue. Acts 18 tells the story of the first Corinthian church.

Read Acts 18:1-11

- ❓ *What is Paul's mission strategy (v 1-6)?*
- ❓ *Where does opposition come from (v 5-6)?*
- ❓ *Why does Paul stay so long (v 9-10)? What effect do you think 18 months of Paul's teaching would have had on the new Corinthian church?*

Paul preaches the gospel for as long as possible to anyone who will listen. Before financial help arrives from Macedonia, he's busy tent-making six days a week and spending his day off (Saturday) at the synagogue. Then when the Jews reject him, he doesn't turn tail and run away—he switches focus to the Gentiles instead, investing a huge amount of time in discipling them.

Mission stopped?

Read Acts 18:12-18a

- ❓ *What is darkly comical about this scene?*
- ❓ *What is Gallio's attitude to Paul and Sosthenes?*
- ❓ *What three different responses have we seen to the gospel in this chapter?*

Some respond with outright hatred, and others accept the message gladly, but Gallio is indifferent, not interested in the truth—he just wants to avoid trouble.

- ❓ *What clues have we been given about what the Corinthian church was like?*

There's the odd Jew and some God-fearing Greeks, but many are from a pagan background, steeped in idol worship, cult prostitution and superstition. And, as we'll see, they're surrounded by people who want to pull them back to their old ways of life.

⌃ Pray

In what ways do you feel the tug of the surrounding culture, pulling you away from Jesus? Pray that God would use our time in 1 Corinthians to strengthen your roots in him so that you are equipped to resist the tug.

Pray for someone you know in each category: those who hate the gospel, those who are responding joyfully and those who seem indifferent.

Good news first

How do you recognise a genuine believer? What kind of things might make you suspect someone wasn't a real Christian?

Identity check

Some time after Paul left Corinth, he wrote a first letter to the Corinthians (1 Corinthians 5:9), but this letter, in God's sovereignty, has been lost. The Corinthians replied to Paul's letter but demonstrated a serious lack of understanding in certain areas, and so Paul wrote the letter we know as 1 Corinthians in order to address these concerns. It's wonderfully practical because many of the issues facing the Corinthians are the same as those facing us today:

- Does sexual purity really matter?
- How should we treat Christians who have different opinions to us?
- What are spiritual gifts, and how should we use them?
- Does it matter whether the resurrection really happened or not?

But it can also sound like quite a harsh letter because Paul is horrified at some of the things they've been getting up to. That's why these 9 verses are so important to read first!

Read 1 Corinthians 1:1-3

- ❓ *What do we learn about Paul?*
- ❓ *What do we learn about the Corinthians?*
- ❓ *Why are these things important to remember as we go on?*

Paul isn't writing this letter off the top of his head. His words come with the authority of Christ. Ignoring the apostle is not an option. The Corinthians (and we) might not always like what he says, but they need to wrestle with it! And that's because they're genuine Christians, made holy by faith in Jesus' blood. This letter is all about helping them to act in line with their true identity.

Abundant grace
Read 1 Corinthians 1:4-9

- ❓ *Why does Paul always give thanks for them (v 4)?*
- ❓ *How is God's grace seen in their lives (v 5-9)?*

Paul isn't thanking the Corinthians for all these good things, nor is he flattering them—he's thanking God, because any and every good fruit in our lives flows directly from his grace.

▾ Apply

- ❓ *What examples of God's grace in your life are you particularly thankful for at the moment?*
- ❓ *How good are you at remembering that these things are a gift and not something you have earned?*

How wonderful that our salvation is not dependent on how well we measure up but on the unchanging faithfulness of our Saviour. Come to him now in repentance, faith and thankfulness.

Divided by pride

After the hugely positive start to the letter, Paul launches straight into tackling a major heart issue.

Superiority complex
Read 1 Corinthians 1:10-12

- ❷ *What is the nature of the problem that Paul is addressing here?*
- ❷ *Why does Paul rebuke those who are saying, "I follow Christ" along with everyone else, do you think?*

After Paul visited Corinth, so did both Apollos (Acts 19:1) and Peter (1 Corinthians 9:5). But instead of rejoicing at the richness of the teaching they've received, the Corinthians are locked in a futile argument about which "celebrity Christian" is the best. The "I follow Christ" party are part of the problem too; by claiming to be above all this petty squabbling, they're actually joining in, trying to win "holy points".

⌄ Apply

- ❷ *Why do we find it so easy to split into groups and quarrel with each other, do you think?*
- ❷ *How do you see this in your society, your friendships and your church?*

We see it in politics, in the playground and in the pew. We love to be in the "best" group, confident that we're right and everyone else is wrong. And we love to put people down, whether openly or subtly: "I told you my way would be quicker!" "Did you really think that was a good sermon?" "I always make my own gravy…" It makes us feel secure and superior, like little gods, reigning supreme.

Christ supreme
Read 1 Corinthians 1:13-17

- ❷ *How does Paul suggest the Corinthians deal with the problem (see v 10)?*
- ❷ *What motivation does Paul give them for these actions (v 13-17)?*
- ❷ *So what might it look like to disagree well?*

This church has completely lost their focus on Christ, instead devoting themselves to petty one-upmanship. Paul reminds them that they're all on the same team—and it's the winning team: the team of Christ's cross. How quickly our disagreements vanish in the light of Jesus' sacrifice for us. It's not that the Corinthians are all to be carbon copies of each other, but that their prideful, divided hearts are to be humble and united around their precious Saviour. Likewise, it's ok to think that one preacher/author/style of music/style of church is more helpful than another, so long as we accept that others have a different viewpoint and we're prepared to submit to them out of love.

⌃ Pray

Pray for someone in your church family with whom you don't always see eye to eye, that your differences would be overcome by the unity of the cross.

Bible in a year: 2 Chronicles 23-24 • Luke 9 v 18-36

Fooling ourselves

Our modern use of the word "fool" can hide from us the seriousness of what Proverbs reveals about a person who ignores God and damages themselves and others.

Mark all the verses that refer to foolishness as you...

Read Proverbs 17

> ❷ *Now, go through the verses you have marked and ask the following questions:*
> • *What would a fool look like in this situation—how do I spot one?*
> • *What effect do they have on themselves?*
> • *What effect do they have on others?*
> • *What hope is there for them?*

Disguise

It's not necessarily that easy to spot a fool. They can appear intelligent (v 28) by sitting quietly and nodding sagely at the conversation, and may also be interested in lots of things (v 24). But what they lack is a focus on the important things of life. If they had the cash to spare, they would not choose to spend it on wisdom (v 16). They may be without a care in the world and seemingly "free", but actually, because they ignore God, they are enslaved.

> ❷ *Do any people you know fit into this category?*
> ❷ *Why is it helpful to see that the Bible calls them fools?*

Damage

> ❷ *Look over the verses you marked again and work out who and what is damaged by a fool.*

Again, a fool may look harmless enough, but don't be deceived (v 12). They are more dangerous than an enraged bear protecting her cubs. Fools often love to catch us up in their ideas and schemes, and we have been warned not to walk with them in their folly.

But fools also do untold damage to families. Pain, grief and bitterness often come to their parents (v 21, 25). Children should be a joy and delight, which makes the experience of having a foolish son or daughter all the more hurtful.

Disaster
Re-read Proverbs 17:10

Fools simply do not learn. How can anyone change, or see their need for change, when they are unable to take or properly respond to criticism of any kind?

⌃ Pray

Think of families known to you who are grieving a child who has wandered from the Lord.

Pray that God would grant repentance and faith to the children, and patient prayerfulness to the parents.

Then pray that you would have eyes to see, humility to admit and strength to change any foolish ways that you're following in your own life.

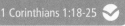

Fools for Christ

Remember how, back in Acts 18, we saw very different responses to the gospel? The section from 1 Corinthians 1:18 up to the end of chapter 2 explains why this happens.

The Corinthians really valued wisdom. There were a lot of talented philosophers plying their trade in Corinth, which had led the Christians to think that they'd gone beyond what Paul had taught them—the apparently simple truths of the gospel.

Dead end

Read 1 Corinthians 1:18-23

- ❷ *What do the non-Christians you know think about the message of the cross?*
- ❷ *How does verse 18 describe non-Christian responses to the cross?*
- ❷ *How does it make you feel when people ridicule your faith?*

Non-Christians might be very polite about it, but we've probably all faced incredulous looks and sniggers when people find out that yes, we really do believe that God sent his Son to die for us! It can be so frustrating when this beautiful truth, the jewel at the centre of our whole lives, is treated as a fairytale at best, and at worst as an offensive delusion of the weak-minded.

- ❷ *So why is the message of the cross foolishness to unbelievers?*
  - *v 19-21*
  - *v 22-23*

No matter how clever or educated we are, it will never be possible for us to reach God by ourselves. He is our infinite, eternal Creator; he's holding all the cards. The Jews thought they could "follow the signs", but a

crucified, servant Messiah wasn't their idea of a conquering king, and so they stumbled over Jesus—they lost their way and lost their Messiah. The Greeks thought their brain-power would lead them to the truth, but a dead God looks like folly to every person who is relying on their non-Spirit-informed reason—how could that be part of an good, wise, eternal plan?

···· TIME OUT ···

Read Isaiah 29:13-16

- ❷ *What is the people's attitude towards God here?*
- ❷ *Why is this so ridiculous?*

God's call

Read 1 Corinthians 1:24-25

- ❷ *Why is the cross wisdom to believers?*

It's all about God's initiative. Only with his intervention will what looks like a foolish plan make perfect sense and the weakness of the cross be revealed as stronger than sin, death and the devil. Human wisdom can never understand or add to this.

🔼 Pray

Do you remember a time when the cross seemed foolish to you? Praise God for revealing the truth to you, and ask that you would never pridefully think you've outgrown it.

Glory thieves

Have you ever been tempted to take the credit—the glory—for something you've not actually done? An idea at work, perhaps, or a kind deed or funny joke?

Well, the Corinthians were stealing glory from God.

The Corinthians = nothing

Read 1 Corinthians 1:26-31

❓ *What eight unflattering characteristics does Paul apply to the Corinthians in verses 26-28? What is his point?*

❓ *What is God's purpose in doing things in this unexpected way (v 29-31)?*

Paul is reminding the Corinthians who they really are: nobodies in the eyes of the world and chosen by God purely because of his grace, not because they deserve it. In fact, you could almost say that God chose them because they were so foolish, weak and insignificant, so it would be obvious that he's the one taking all the initiative and the one deserving of all the glory.

⌃ Pray

❓ *How does this challenge you? Are you ever tempted to think that God chose you because, actually, you're great?*

Confess your glory-hunger, and then humbly praise him for Jesus' gift of righteousness, holiness and redemption (v 30), which changes you from a nobody into a precious child of the King.

Paul = nothing

Read 1 Corinthians 2:1-5

❓ *How does Paul use verses 1-4 to prove verse 5 to the Corinthians?*

Paul didn't preach in a flashy, well-oiled way—he wasn't like the great rhetoricians who toured the region. Instead he was weak, fearful and trembling. Yet, the Corinthians believed! It must have been God!

❓ *Can you think of any other biblical examples of God working in this unexpected way?*

They're everywhere! God chose the elderly, barren Abraham and Sarah to be the ancestors of his people. He gave puny David victory over the fearsome Goliath. He filled 5000 people with just five loaves and two fish. It would have been farcical for Abraham and Sarah, David or the little boy to take the glory for these things. Instead, they could rejoice in being used by God to display his beautiful, glorious grace.

⌄ Apply

❓ *Do you ever try to hide your weaknesses and present a strong, wise, got-it-together front so that people will attribute any success you have to your own abilities?*

❓ *How could you make it more obvious to non-believers that God is behind every blessing you have?*

The spectacular Spirit

How often do you think about the Holy Spirit? If, like me, you sometimes take him for granted, prepare to have your eyes opened!

Mystery revealed…
Read 1 Corinthians 2:6-8

❓ *What is the essential content of this message of wisdom which Paul is talking about (see 1:18)?*

❓ *Who is Paul talking about in 2:6 and 8?*

❓ *How is this another example of the strong being shamed by the weak?*

The cross of Christ is the focal point of history and of God's eternal rescue plan. The Jewish leaders and Pilate used their "wisdom" to brutally murder the only truly innocent man who has ever existed—but in doing so, they opened the door to forgiveness and eternal life.

❓ *Re-read verse 7. How does it make you feel?*

Before creation, God had already planned that through Jesus' death, you would be one of those destined for eternal glory. Mind-boggling!

… by the Spirit
Read 1 Corinthians 2:9-16

❓ *What is the role of the Holy Spirit in enabling us to understand the gospel?*
- *v 9-10a*   • *v 10b-12*
- *v 13*

God's Spirit—the Holy Spirit—is God himself, and so he comprehends fully all of God's thoughts (v 11). And, mind-blowingly,

it's this same Spirit that is in us, enabling us to understand all that God wishes to reveal to us (v 12)! In fact, this is the only way the message of the cross can make sense to us.

❓ *What is the contrast in verses 14-16?*

❓ *Why should we not be discouraged when non-Christians ridicule us?*

The words for "discern" and "judge" in verses 14 and 15 are the same. Those with the Spirit are able to "discern" all things— able to distinguish clearly truth from error, wisdom from folly, right from wrong—because God is giving them the ability. This is in contrast to the person in verse 14, who lacks this spiritual discernment. And those with the Spirit are above mere human judgements because the Spirit is infinitely wiser than even the wisest mere human. Through the Spirit, we have the wisdom of God—access to the very "mind of Christ" (v 16)!

❓ *What difference will remembering this make next time you are ridiculed for your faith?*

🔼 Pray

Praise God for his eternal plan to send his Spirit into your mind and show you the wisdom of the cross. Ask that he would do the same for those around you who don't understand who Jesus is and why he died.

A measure of maturity

After the spiritual high at the end of chapter 2, we're back down to earth with a bump.

Infants in Christ

The Corinthians thought of themselves as mature, influential Christians and prided themselves on their spiritual gifts.

Read 1 Corinthians 3:1-4

> ❷ *What were the Corinthians like when Paul first met them?*
> ❷ *What are they like now? What reason does Paul give (v 3)?*

It's pretty startling, isn't it? The Corinthians would have been crushed when they read this. They've made hardly any spiritual progress! They, who think themselves so mature, are spiritually stunted because of their prideful disagreements.

> ❷ *How seriously does God take jealousy and quarrelling?*
> ❷ *What do they reveal about our hearts—about what we're trusting?*

When we jostle for position, frantically trying to climb higher up the ladder than those around us, we're taking God completely out of the equation. We're indistinguishable from those caught in the rat race, whose only hope in life is being "better" than other people.

···· **TIME OUT** ·································

The Corinthians had benefited from 18 months of Paul's teaching. In contrast, the Thessalonians only got about two weeks.

Read 1 Thessalonians 1:2-10

> ❷ *How is Paul's assessment of the Thessalonians different from what he says about the Corinthians?*

It's possible for a new Christian—a spiritual baby—to show more fruit and be growing towards maturity much faster than a hard-hearted, proud person who's been a believer for years.

How things grow

Paul now helps the Corinthians to insert God back into the equation.

Read 1 Corinthians 3:5-9

> ❷ *How does Paul help the Corinthians to see their leaders rightly?*

Paul likens this church to a field. He and Apollos are mere labourers; it's God who turns the barren field into a harvest! You wouldn't praise a car for giving you a lift! So instead of quarrelling about who is the best, the Corinthians should humbly praise God, who has given them everything.

☑ Apply

> ❷ *Do you think of yourself as a spiritual baby or an adult? How do you know which you are?*
> ❷ *What kind of Christian are you more impressed by: one who is confident, knowledgeable, outgoing, wealthy... or who displays the fruit of the Spirit (Galatians 5:22-23)?*

The leaders we need

After rebuking the Corinthians about their attitude to their leaders yesterday, Paul now helps them to recognise what makes a good leader.

Warning: builders!
Read 1 Corinthians 3:10-17

- ❷ How does Paul use the building metaphor to describe what has been going on in Corinth (v 10)?
- ❷ What must the foundation be made from (v 11)?
- ❷ Which of the materials in verse 12 will withstand the fire?
- ❷ What will happen to the "builder" whose work doesn't survive (v 15)?

Paul is warning the Corinthians about the leaders who have come after him, who are building on the solid, Christ-centred foundation he laid. Some of them are building well, but many are building badly—with materials which will perish on judgment day. The leaders themselves will be saved, so long as they are indeed trusting in Christ, but their ministry will prove fruitless.

- ❷ What is the warning in verses 16-17?

God really loves his church, and he dwells in it by his Spirit. If a leader is so corrupt as to spiritually destroy the church, then he also will be destroyed. This was a real danger in Corinth because the leaders had become so obsessed with "wisdom" that they'd forgotten the heart of the gospel.

⌄ Apply

- ❷ What would it look like in real life for a leader in your church to build well?

- ❷ What would it look like for someone involved in a ministry to build badly? How could they do this without anyone really noticing?
- ❷ How does this challenge you as a congregation member? As a leader?

Truly wise
Read 1 Corinthians 3:18-23

These verses neatly summarise what we've learnt in the last three chapters. In the world's eyes, giving up control of our lives to an invisible God is pure folly. But it's only when we recognise the inability of our own wisdom to bring us lasting satisfaction, and we humbly acknowledge his lordship, that we truly begin to know wisdom.

- ❷ How do verses 21-23 put the Corinthians' petty one-upmanship into perspective?

The God who controls life, death and all of time and space graciously gives us everything we need, because we belong to him in Christ. Boasting has no place before him.

⌃ Pray

Ask God to expand your view of the truth of verse 23. Then pray through your answers to the Apply questions above.

The verdict on you

What's your real opinion of yourself, deep down? Think about who you are and how you're doing. Do you feel pleased, downhearted or conflicted?

Well, our passage today shows us a better way to evaluate yourself—asking a different question.

Whose verdict?

Read 1 Corinthians 4:1-5

Here in chapter 4, Paul is reminding the Corinthians of his authority as an apostle and admonishing them for their worldly arrogance in thinking they could go beyond the truth he's taught them.

> ❷ *How do verses 1-2 remind us of the role and responsibility of leaders seen in chapter 3?*

Paul has shown the Corinthians that he's been building well on the foundation of Christ, and so they should respect him as God's faithful servant. But they don't. So he now goes on to explain his own personal attitude towards their poor opinion of him.

> ❷ *Whose opinion doesn't matter to Paul (4:3)?*
> ❷ *Whose opinion does matter (v 4-5)?*

Don't miss how revolutionary this is. Paul isn't trapped by agonising people-pleasing. His identity isn't wrapped up in how well he thinks he's doing. He's free. With God in his rightful place as Lord of Paul's life, no one else's opinion matters.

> ❷ *And what is God's opinion of Paul, and us (see Romans 8:1)?*

We've got the thumbs-up from the King of the universe. That's a truth powerful enough to dispel every other judgement ever made on us.

☑ Apply

> ❷ *How would your life be different if, like Paul, you focused on how God sees you through Jesus, rather than on how others see you or how you see yourself?*

Gifts from above

Paul doesn't care what the Corinthians think of him for his own sake, but he does care for their sake. By rejecting him, they're rejecting God's truth and instead following wrong beliefs. So he reminds them of the foolishness of their superiority complex.

Read 1 Corinthians 4:6-7

> ❷ *What do you think Paul means by "what is written" (v 6)? How does this protect us from false teaching?*
> ❷ *How is v 7 a beautiful antidote to pride?*

Everything we have is a gift from God. Our abilities, our families, our jobs, our faith—all of it is pure, undeserved grace.

☑ Pray

Are you feeling down on yourself? Pray for God's verdict to carry the weight it should. Are you, to be honest, feeling proud? Pray for a humble, grateful heart which acknowledges that everything you have is from him.

Heat-seeking missiles

Like rich, fine food, proverbs are best consumed in small quantities. And they can act like heat-seeking missiles, zooming in on an immediate problem.

Not every proverb is appropriate for the moment. But when the time or the situation is right, one of God's wise, insightful sayings will shed light on a situation and maybe even offer a valuable key to open a locked door.

Read Proverbs 17 again—focusing on the verses we have not covered in the previous two sessions. Ask the following questions, and write the verse out in your own words underneath:

- ❓ *Which of these proverbs strikes you as particularly important or relevant for someone you know who is in a difficult situation?*

- ❓ *Which of these proverbs addresses a problem you have at your church at the moment?*

- ❓ *Which of these proverbs do you most need to heed yourself right now?*

⌄ Apply

Think carefully how you might communicate the truths you have seen today to the people you are concerned about.

- ❓ *Will you write a note to them?*
- ❓ *Will you determine to have an open, caring conversation with them?*
- ❓ *Will you speak to someone in church leadership about how to speak with them?*
- ❓ *Will you talk with a close friend about the challenge you have personally received from God's word today?*

Determine to follow through on these thoughts. Make a note in your diary to make sure you do not forget.

⌃ Pray

Before you do any of those things, however, pray for the people concerned—your friend, your church, yourself.

Ask the Lord to guide you in what might be, perhaps, a difficult conversation.

Ask the Lord to give you a heart that is open to rebuke and repentance.

Ask the Holy Spirit to do his work in your heart and the hearts of others to make you more like Jesus.

Successful ministry

What would you say characterises a successful ministry? Growth? A good reputation? Impactful, exciting services? A large staff team?

Comic contrast

To help the Corinthians to see the ridiculousness of their arrogance, Paul sets up an ironic contrast.

Read 1 Corinthians 4:8-13

- ❷ *How does Paul describe the way the Corinthians see themselves (v 8, 10)?*
- ❷ *How does he contrast this with himself and the other apostles (v 9-13)?*
- ❷ *How should this make the Corinthians re-evaluate what "success" is?*

While the Corinthians are prancing around like kings, believing they've arrived at the pinnacle of wisdom and spirituality, the apostles are the most despised spectacle imaginable—like those at the end of a Roman procession who are about to be publicly executed (which many of them were). Paul's point is that if the apostles are living like this, and they're the ones whom Jesus appointed to found the church, then surely suffering is the norm for Christians. The Corinthians shouldn't be embarrassed by Paul or look down on him because he's suffering. Instead, they should be challenged to be like him—to put the cross of Christ above their comfort, their reputation and their flashy new leaders: above everything.

▾ Apply

- ❷ *If you were to list the things which characterised your life, would your list look more like: Paul's or that of the Corinthians? How does this challenge you?*

Love hurts

Read 1 Corinthians 4:14-21

- ❷ *What is Paul's motivation for saying these rather harsh words (v 14-15)?*
- ❷ *What is Paul's plan to help the Corinthians get back on track (v 16, 17, 19, 21)?*

Paul isn't having a go at them because he's fed up with and hurt by their abuse. He's acting out of genuine, agonised love, as their spiritual father. He longs for them to flourish! He's even sent Timothy to help them, probably at great personal cost.

- ❷ *What does Paul hope to prove when he visits Corinth (v 18-20)?*

It sounds as if there might be a bit of a showdown with some of the dodgy leaders; they talk the talk but don't actually have the Spirit's power, and so they'll be unmasked.

- ❷ *How does God define "successful" ministry (see v 2)?*

Faithfulness to the gospel of the cross is more important than eloquence or wisdom or charisma or a large congregation or lots of money.

- ❷ *How does this encourage you in your personal evangelism?*

The sin among you

After four chapters of wrangling about wisdom, foolishness, leaders and divisions, Paul now begins to deal with some tricky issues of church discipline.

Sin is deadly
Read 1 Corinthians 5:1-5

- ❓ *What sin has the man committed (v 1)?*
- ❓ *How have the Corinthians sinfully responded to his sin (v 2)?*
- ❓ *What does this tell us about their view of sin?*

A Christian man is having an affair with his step-mother (see Leviticus 18:8). It's so bad that even the pagans knew it was a no-no—and they permitted just about anything! But, as we'll see later, this church seems to think that, as Christians, we can do whatever we like because we're free from the law and saved by grace. They may even have been proud of their inclusiveness.

- ❓ *What does Paul tell them to do about this problem (1 Corinthians 5:2)?*
- ❓ *How are they to go about doing this (v 3-5)?*
- ❓ *What is the hoped-for result (v 5)?*

These are difficult verses, both to understand and apply. But it's important to keep the ultimate aim in mind (v 5). Paul cares deeply about this man and about the church. The aim of casting the man out of the fellowship is that he will hopefully be shocked to his senses and recognise his sin for what it is—his "flesh" (his sinful nature) will be destroyed. This will enable him to repent, return to the fellowship and ultimately be saved.

⌄ Apply

- ❓ *How do we see a Corinthian attitude to sin in the church today?*

Our prevailing culture is one where tolerance has been elevated above pretty much everything else, and that filters into the church. It's much easier to make excuses and turn a blind eye to sin than confront someone. More on this in the next study, but...

- ❓ *Is there anyone you need to speak to about their sin—or anyone you need to listen to about yours—today?*

Sin spreads
Read 1 Corinthians 5:6-8

- ❓ *What do the yeast and the dough represent?*

Before Passover, the Jews cleared out all their old yeast and made unleavened bread for a week. Then they'd start afresh with new yeast after Passover. Paul is saying that Jesus' death has inaugurated a fresh start—the old yeast of sin is gone. Why would we let it back in? And if we do, it'll spread like wildfire through the whole church: "She's getting away with it, so why can't I?"

⌃ Pray

Pray for your church family, that you would be united in stopping sin in its tracks.

Bible in a year: Haggai · Luke 14 v 1-24

Deal with sin

Following on from his warnings to the church about the sin they're tolerating, Paul now instructs the church on how to deal with sin in general.

Last resort
Read 1 Corinthians 5:9-11 and Matthew 18:15-17

❷ *What is Paul's command in 1 Corinthians 5:9 and 11?*

❷ *How does Jesus' teaching in Matthew 18 explain the stages which lead up to this exclusion from the fellowship?*

❷ *What do you think Paul means by "do not even eat with such people"?*

Does Paul mean that as soon as anyone glares at you as you park your car, or forgets to give you back your pen, you should cut off all contact with them? Of course not: there'd soon be no church left! He's talking about unrepentant sin. If anyone claims to be a Christian but wilfully continues in sin after warnings from a friend, from additional witnesses and from the church as a whole, then the only option is to expel them from the fellowship. We're not even to eat with them—which may simply mean we're not to have them round for meals in a friendly way, or it might be a reference to eating the Lord's Supper with them, or both.

❷ *How does 1 Corinthians 15:6-8 help to explain why Paul takes this line?*

Sin is like norovirus. For the sake of the whole church, it must be purged.

❷ *What exception does verse 10 make?*

It's completely fine to associate with non-Christians who are doing these things—Jesus certainly did! We are to be salt and light in the world! How would anyone become a Christian if we could never speak to them?

✓ Apply

❷ *If you're in church leadership: how does your church do what Paul encourages here? What might stop you doing it?*

❷ *If you're a church member: how do/ should you support your leaders in leading your church this way?*

Right and wrong judging
Read 1 Corinthians 5:12-13

❷ *Which people are we to judge? Why (see above)?*

❷ *Who are we not to judge? Why?*

❷ *Why do we so often get this the wrong way round?*

As a church, we should be pointing out each other's sin; this is the most loving response, designed to be remedial rather than punitive. We should not be pointing out the sin of unbelievers—how can they live Jesus' way when they have no knowledge of his saving grace and lack his Holy Spirit? Yet so often, we are accepting of sin in the church and judgmental of those outside.

❷ *Can you think of an example of this in your own church and your own culture?*

See you out of court

How do you resolve a sibling argument over the remote? You definitely don't take it to court! (Do you?!)

A thorny problem
Read 1 Corinthians 6:1-6

> ❓ *What problem is Paul addressing (v 1, 6)?*
> ❓ *What's the irony (v 4)?*

Just like any family, the church family will experience disputes. But there's been a severe overreaction in Corinth, which is reflecting badly on the gospel. Their disputes are probably connected with money and property, as Paul mentions being cheated in verse 7. In other words, these are issues which it is possible to settle "out of court"— not crimes like murder or abuse, which require the civil authorities to step in.

But these Christians are so incapable of sorting it out themselves that they're asking those still walking in darkness to enlighten them!

> ❓ *How does Paul help the Corinthians to see how ridiculous they're being (v 2-3, 4-5)?*

On the last day, the church will be involved in Jesus' final judgment of all things. We don't know exactly what that entails, but surely if we're going to take part in that great judgment, we should be able to manage comparatively trivial cases in the meantime! We have God's wisdom—why would we go to those outside the church, who only have human wisdom?

A radical solution
Read 1 Corinthians 6:7-8

> ❓ *What do these lawsuits reveal about the Corinthians' spiritual health (v 7a, 8)?*
> ❓ *What better option does Paul suggest (v 7b)?*

"My rights" has defeated unity. Selfishness has defeated love. But in Jesus' kingdom, it's the meek, the merciful and the peacemakers who are blessed (Matthew 5:3-12).

> ❓ *Why is it so difficult to resolve differences, even (or especially) with other Christians?*

God's standards are infinitely higher than those of human courts. The onus is on us to be Christ-like, and that involves sacrificial forgiveness. We can only do this by looking at what Jesus did for us on the cross.

✓ Apply

> ❓ *When you feel wronged by another Christian, how do you tend to react— both internally and externally?*
> ❓ *When might it be right to stand your ground and appeal to church leadership?*
> ❓ *When might it be right to quietly stand down, giving up your rights for the sake of unity and church witness?*

Pray that God's wisdom would fill you as you seek to glorify him in any disputes you are involved in or witnessing.

But you were washed

Have you ever thought, "I'm just going to go ahead and sin: God will forgive me later"?

Who are you?
Read 1 Corinthians 6:9-11

❓ *How do these verses follow on from verse 8? Who are the "wrongdoers" (v 9)?*

❓ *What is Paul's warning?*

❓ *Does this mean that if we do any of these things, we're excluded from God's kingdom, do you think?*

The issue here is, again, *persistent, unrepentant* sin. The Corinthians are still acting in the same way they did before they became Christians. This is extremely dangerous. If their behaviour is indistinguishable from the world, then are they true believers at all?

❓ *How do the three truths of verse 11 help us to hate our sin?*

• *We've been washed: our sin is gone; we are free from guilt and clean in God's sight.*

• *We've been sanctified: made holy, set apart to live for him.*

• *We've been justified: declared right before God because Jesus has taken the punishment for our sin.*

This is who we are. Sin is incompatible with this identity. It's like being given expensive new clothes for a wedding and immediately ruining them by rolling in a pig sty.

☑ Apply

Meditate on how these three glorious truths extinguish your love of sin.

❓ *In what one specific area do these truths most need to go to work in you, so that you would fight your sin more fiercely?*

Sex and society

In the next passage, Paul will focus in on the area of sexual immorality (v 12-20). Corinth was a pagan city where promiscuousness was viewed as perfectly good and normal—you could sleep with other people's spouses, men, women, prostitutes... anyone you fancied. It would have been really difficult for new converts to get used to God's way of living.

Re-read 1 Corinthians 6:9

Sexual immorality, adultery and homosexual practice are all listed separately.

❓ *How could you use this to gently show someone that sex outside of marriage, no matter how committed, is disobedient to God?*

Our society generally frowns on adultery, but any other loving, committed relationship between adults is applauded, and marriage seen as completely unnecessary. Yet the Bible calls all sex outside of heterosexual marriage "sexual immorality". Have you ever wished it didn't? Life would be so much easier if God's standards were the same as ours! *But if we only obey him when we agree with him, then we're not really obeying him at all.*

Your body matters

Why is sexual immorality such a big deal? Because of what you body is, and who it belongs to.

Excuses, excuses
Read 1 Corinthians 6:12-13

❓ *What two excuses are being used to justify sexual immorality (Paul quotes them in v 12 and 13a)?*

❓ *How does Paul show them that they're getting it wrong (v 12a, 12b, 13b)?*

According to the Corinthians, being saved by faith alone means we have the right to do whatever we like with our bodies. But Paul reminds them that because of Jesus' death for us (v 11), we are bound to a much higher standard—if anything is unhelpful for godliness, or in danger of drawing us away from Christ, we must reject it!

Secondly, in verse 13, the Corinthians were being influenced by the Greek idea that the body is "bad"—only the soul matters and is eternal. Surely sex is just an appetite to be satisfied! But Paul points out that the body has a much higher purpose than eating or sex—it's for the Lord, and so what we do with it matters hugely.

Honour God!

But Paul's not finished! He goes on to give several more reasons why bodies matter.

Read 1 Corinthians 6:14-20

❓ *How does Paul correct the "Greek" understanding of the body (v 14)?*

Newsflash: our bodies are eternal! The same body we have now will be raised up and live for ever, just like Jesus' body. We will be changed, glorified and freed from sin, but still recognisably *us*. What we do with our bodies now matters.

❓ *What is the unresolvable tension in verses 15-17?*

As Christians, our bodies are joined to Christ (see Colossians 3:1-4). But in sexual immorality, our bodies are joined to a "prostitute"/a person we're not married to. There's a dangerous incompatibility there.

❓ *In what way is sexual sin self-destructive (1 Corinthians 6:18)?*

There's no such thing as casual sex. When two become one flesh, there's a spiritual connection. Ripping that apart is soul-destroying, whether we realise it or not.

❓ *Why else should we "honour God with [our] bodies" (v 19-20)?*

It's as if our bodies are on loan from God, like a really precious library book. We need to bring them back to him in as good a condition as possible!

⌄ Apply

❓ *What changes do you need to make to help you to flee from sexual immorality (in your thought life, what you watch, your actions)?*

We'll return to 1 Corinthians after Christmas...

Lips and ears

You've probably heard this sound advice: God gave you two ears and one mouth, so listen twice as much as you speak. That's what we will focus on in today's reading.

As you read through the verses, mark the ones that you think are particularly appropriate for you at the moment.

Read Proverbs 18:1-21

Lips

Re-read Proverbs 18:4, 6-8, 13, 17

❓ *Which of these verses do you find particularly striking or surprising?*

There's some great advice for talkers here. Notice how it is the effect that words have that show whether the speaker is wise or foolish (v 4). The words may be high-sounding, seem profound, or appear to be sensible, but people can still drown in what is being said. Genuinely wise words, on the other hand, will be as pure and refreshing as a bubbling brook.

Ears

Re-read Proverbs 18:2, 13, 17

Foolish lips and minds are often a result of closed ears. The person who is too full of their own opinions to listen to others is a fool in God's sight (v 2, 13). And sometimes we need to listen even though we're convinced that we know the answer (v 17).

Politicians, pundits, preachers: we all have our favourites. But are we attracted to them based on our prejudices or their ability to sound profound? The *effect* of their words is a good test to apply.

❓ *Politicians: Do their words lead to peace and righteousness?*
❓ *Pundits: Do they mock and denigrate others?*
❓ *Preachers: Do their words stir up love for Jesus and other people?*

☑ Apply

Time to take the *Explore* listening test:

❓ *When a friend tells you about an argument that they've had with someone, do you always take your friends' side?*
❓ *Do you vote the same way you always have?*
❓ *Do you ever answer without listening?*
❓ *Do you enjoy telling others about your opinions?*
❓ *Do you interrupt people in a discussion?*
❓ *At prayer meetings, are you working out what you will pray while someone else is praying?*

⌃ Pray

Read verse 15 and make it the basis of your prayers of confession.

And pray for those politicians, preachers and social-media commentators: that their words would be wise, just and righteous.

CHRISTMAS: Family time

We're all shaped by our families. Some of us are proud of our family; some spend life trying to escape, or live up to, their expectations; others are searching for their family.

By definition, to be human is to be born into a family line. The Lord Jesus was no different. And the kind of family God the Father chose for his Son to be born into tells us a great deal about why he was born at all, what he was like and how we should respond to his birth. This Christmas, we're looking at various members of Jesus' family tree, stretching back through the centuries.

Read Matthew 1:1-17

> ❷ *Why do you think verse 1 picks out these two particular ancestors of Jesus?*

We'll look at the first of these men today and the second tomorrow.

Promise to a king

We are rewinding to about 1,000 BC, in Jerusalem, the new capital of God's people, Israel. David, the anointed king (or, in Hebrew, "messiah"), is considering building a permanent home—a temple—for God.

Read 2 Samuel 7:4-17

> ❷ *What has God done for David and the people he rules (v 8-11a)?*
> ❷ *What will God do for David (v 11b-13)?*
> ❷ *How will God relate to this descendant of David (v 14-15)?*

David was a messiah of his people—but here God promises *the* Messiah: a King who will rule for ever... who will in some special sense be God's own Son... who will face difficulty, but who will never lose the love of

God or the throne of God's kingdom.

We can imagine residents of the royal palace looking into the crib of every baby boy born in the royal line and thinking, *Could he be the one?* And—though partial fulfilment came through Solomon, David's son—ultimately the answer was always *No.* Until Christmas. Until "the birth of Jesus the Messiah came about" (Matthew 1:18).

Response of a king
Read 2 Samuel 7:18-29

> ❷ *What is the tone of David's response, when it comes to his view of...*
> • *himself?* • *his God?*

Who am I ... that you have brought me this far? There is awed amazement here, that God would bring David into his purposes; that God would use him in bringing his Messiah into the world. And we can echo this, for we have likewise been brought in. **Read Ephesians 1:3-6.** How humbling to know that the God of the universe has chosen, for no discernible reason, to bring us not only into his family but also into his purposes to glorify his Messiah in his world.

⌃ Pray

Who am I, that you have brought me this far? Praise God for your place in his family. Praise him for your King, the Lord Jesus. Praise him that his kingdom is everlasting.

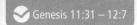

Abraham: the obedience

Jesus is the son of David, inheriting and fulfilling those messianic promises. But the promises he fulfils go far further back in history, for he is also "the son of Abraham".

Go, Abram*

Read Genesis 11:31 – 12:1-3

- ❓ *What command does God give Abram?*
- ❓ *What promises does God give him?*
- ❓ *What information about the land does God give him?*
- ❓ *What was Abram being called to leave in order to go?*

Someone once said that the Bible can be divided into two parts: Genesis 1 – 12:3 and Genesis 12:4 – Revelation 22. Everything that happens in the rest of Scripture is the story of how God fulfilled his promises to Abram: promises of a great nation descended from him, blessed by God, settled in God-given land and bringing blessing to peoples all over the earth. People, land, blessing... At every stage in the Old Testament, it's helpful to ask, "How well are the promises going?" At times, they were partially fulfilled—at many other times, including zero BC, they must have seemed little more than a tragic joke. As Jesus was born, the descendants of Abraham were riven by factions, decimated by exile and war, arguing about who God was and under Roman occupation. And yet Matthew invites his Jewish audience a few decades later to peer into the manger of a shack in Bethlehem and say, *Here is the son of Abraham. Here is the way the promises are fulfilled.*

Of course, in Genesis 12 Abram knew none of that as he considered his response to

God's call to leave everything he knew, and almost everyone he knew, and travel to an as-yet unidentified land.

And so Abram…

Read Genesis 12:4-7

- ❓ *What is impressive about Abram's response?*
- ❓ *Imagine you had been living in Haran as Abram prepared to go. What might you have thought of his decision?*

Don't underestimate the faith that lay behind the first three words of verse 4: "So Abram went". From the outset, Jesus' family had been a people who based their lives on God keeping his promises. Jesus himself would have to entrust his spirit to his Father, trusting that death was not the end (Luke 23:46). This is the engine of the obedience God calls for: he says, "Go", he makes great promises to us... and then our part is to obey, and join the adventure.

⌄ Apply

- ❓ *Is there something that God is calling you to, that you're stalling on or trying to avoid?*
- ❓ *What promise of God would help you to obey, if you lived as though it is true?*
- ❓ *So... will you now obey?*

* God renamed Abram "Abraham" in Genesis 17:5.

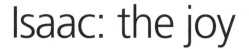

Isaac: the joy

Abram had been promised that God would make his descendants a "great nation". There was just one problem. He couldn't have any—his wife, Sarah, was infertile (11:30).

Contrasting reactions

Read Genesis 15:1-5

Abram is very honest with God (v 2)! He knows that whatever God gives him will also perish with him—including the promises of verse 1, and of 12:2-3.

> ❓ *What does God promise (15:5)? How many details does he give about how he will keep his promise?*

Again, we see that Abram is a man of faith (v 6). Faith does not preclude wrestling, struggling or questioning (v 2); but in the final analysis, faith believes God.

Read Genesis 18:1-2, 9-14

The identity of the "three men" is unclear. They may be angels, speaking for God. Or this may be God himself (v 1). Regardless, they bring a promise, with a detail.

> ❓ *What is it (v 10)?*
> ❓ *What do you make of Sarah's response in verses 11-12?*
> ❓ *What does the LORD seem to make of her response (v 13-14)?*

Enter joy

Read Genesis 21:1-7

> ❓ *How is verse 1 act a kind of spoiler for what we're about to read in verses 2-5?*
> ❓ *How does Sarah respond to the birth of Isaac (v 6-7)?*

A derisory snort in chapter 18, triggered by the physical impossibilities, is replaced by the joyful laugh issuing from divine promise-keeping in chapter 21. This elderly lady's smile as she held her newborn in her arms must have said it all: *God keeps his promises, however unlikely they seem.* God had shown his power through the delivery of an impossible baby—just as he would by causing the conception of Jesus in a virgin's womb centuries later.

And between the births of Sarah's baby and Mary's baby, whenever life grew tough and God seemed distant, Abraham's family could always look back to Isaac and tell each other, "Ah, but God keeps his promises. Smile." And so can we. Smile today. Laugh today. God keeps his promises. God's family is a family of joy.

⌃ Pray

"He who began a good work in you will carry it on to completion until the day of Christ Jesus." (Philippians 1:5)

"Behold, I am with you always." (Matthew 28:20)

"Yes, I am coming soon." (Revelation 22:20)

Ask God to give you faith to believe these promises more and more. Ask for the joy that flows from knowing that God will keep every one of his promises, by his power, in his timing, for your good and his glory.

Boaz: the husband

Earlier in this issue, we covered the lives of Jacob, Judah and Tamar—so we're skipping forward nine generations now, to Boaz.

It's "the days when the judges ruled" (Ruth 1:1). God's people were in the promised land but plagued by their sin and its consequences. **Read Judges 21:25.** And into Israel comes a refugee, a member of the enemy Moabite nation, the widow of an Israelite. Ruth, penniless and hungry, enters one of Boaz's fields to "glean"—to gather the corn dropped by the harvesters, which was God's law allowed her to do (e.g. Leviticus 23:22).

Read Ruth 2:5-9, 14-17

To obey the law (rare, in the days of the Judges), Boaz needed simply to allow Ruth to pick up the unreaped corn at the edges of his fields or the corn dropped by his workers.

❓ *In what ways in these verses does he go beyond what he has to do?*

Read Ruth 2:19-20

❓ *What does Naomi (Ruth's mother-in-law) reveal about Boaz?*

A guardian-redeemer or kinsman-redeemer was obliged to care and provide for any relative who was in serious difficulty—poverty, slavery and so on. It looks as though, in this lawless time, Ruth has found a kinsman-redeemer who will do his duty. So, encouraged by Naomi, she even approaches him to ask him to marry her.

Read Ruth 3:10-13

❓ *How does Boaz feel about Ruth's proposal (v 10-11)?*

This is very kind—he neglects to mention that she is a poverty-stricken Moabite!

❓ *What is the problem, though (v 12)?*

Read Ruth 4:1-10

The closer kinsman-redeemer—the one who has an obligation to help Ruth—refuses to, because while he's happy to have her family land, he's not happy to make any sacrifices or take any risks in order to help her. Boaz, however—who is not under an obligation to do anything—is willing. He will stop at nothing to give Ruth everything. For someone to choose to obey God's law in the days of the judges was remarkable. For someone to choose to go far, far beyond God's law was unimaginable. But Boaz did.

And in this, he points us forward to his far greater descendant...

Read Ephesians 5:25-27 and Revelation 19:6-9

❓ *What has Jesus done as the "husband" of his "bride", the church?*
❓ *Think of the way Boaz treated Ruth. How does it help you to worship Jesus to realise that he treats his people in the same way?*

⬆ Pray

Thank God for Jesus, the greater Boaz. And ask God to make you as generous as your Husband. Who might you offer gleanings—and far more than gleanings—to today?

Rahab: the welcome

Having focused on Boaz, we now turn to enjoy the ways in which God brought his mother into the family line of the Messiah.

Into the family

We're going back a generation. God's people have just entered the promised land, and their first challenge is to take the impregnable high-walled city of Jericho.

Skim-read Joshua 2:1-21

❓ *Why was Rahab an unlikely ally for the Israelite spies?*

❓ *Why, does Rahab say, did she choose to help her people's enemies (v 8-13)?*

Rahab is risking her life—if found out, she will be killed as a traitor. She is staking everything on her belief that the God of Israel is who he says he is, will do what he says he'll do, and will accept a woman with her compromised past.

And wonderfully, he is, and he does, and he will. God demolished the walls and his people took the city. And... **Read Joshua 6:25.** And more than that, Rahab became the great-great-etc. grandmother of the Messiah. There is no one whom God will not welcome if they come in faith. There is no one whom God cannot use as they come in faith.

❓ *How might knowing his mother's history have influenced Rahab's son, Boaz, to act in the way he did towards Ruth?*

▼ Apply

In a sense, you and I are Rahab. By nature we were born outside God's people, "alienated from God and ... enemies in [our] minds because of [our] evil behaviour" (Colossians 1:21). We were born in Jericho. And then, at a particular point in our lives, we heard who God was, we heard what God promises— and we dared to believe that he would accept a person with a sinful nature such as ours. And he did.

❓ *How will knowing your own history influence you to act towards the Ruths around you—those who are physically poor, but perhaps spiritually open?*

❓ *Do you ever think that God could not really use someone like you to do anything special? How does Rahab's presence in Jesus' family tree both encourage and challenge you?*

Rahab's faith

Read Hebrews 11:1, 31

❓ *How did Rahab exemplify the definition of faith that the writer gives us in verse 1? (Use what we've seen in Joshua to help you answer.)*

God's family is a family full of surprising people. They have only one thing in common, but it is the only thing they need: faith in God to be who he says he is and to do what he's said he'll do. *Thank God for giving you that faith, too; and pray that he would point you towards some Rahabs today, to invite them to join the family of God.*

David and Bathsheba

"David was the father of Solomon, whose mother had been Uriah's wife…" (Matthew 1:6). Why not just call her Bathsheba? Matthew's reminding us of a dark family moment.

A #metoo tragedy

Remember who David is: the anointed king, hand-picked by God and the recipient of those wonderful promises (2 Samuel 7).

Read 2 Samuel 11:1-4

> ❓ *What mistakes—or acts of outright disobedience—does David walk through in these verses?*
> ❓ *What amount of choice do you think Bathsheba has here?*

Bathsheba could, in another century, have used the #metoo hashtag.

At work in darkness

Read 2 Samuel 11:5-27

> ❓ *How does David attempt to cover up his sin when he discovers Bathsheba's pregnancy?*
> ❓ *By verse 27's first phrase, how successful have his efforts been?*
> ❓ *What is his only problem (end of v 27)?*

So, in 12:1-14, the prophet Nathan is sent to David. This time, there's no promise of an everlasting kingdom and a greater son; instead, when David confesses what he's done (v 13), he is told that his "utter contempt" means this son of his will not survive.

How do you respond to this? I think we should weep for this child, an innocent victim. We should weep for his mother, now an abuse victim and a widow, grieving a son

and married to her abuser. And we should weep for David. He is repentant and forgiven (read Psalm 51 if you have time); but he has to live with the knowledge of what he has done, and the rest of 2 Samuel details how his family falls apart.

Here is a reminder that Christmas is not a serene fairytale. The thread of God's salvation line was stitched through some dark cloth. But it did not break. God would use this marriage, which began in such horrendous, sinful circumstances, to bring Solomon, the next in the line of Jesus, into the world. No one is too sinful or too broken to be beyond God's forgiveness or healing. And it is because the thread of God's work leads to Jesus, who came "not to call the righteous but sinners" (Mark 2:17), that there can be salvation for sinners—including David, including you and me.

☑ Apply

> ❓ *If you know that you are hiding, ignoring or excusing a sin, how does this passage speak to you?*
> ❓ *If you have a sin in your past that you know you are forgiven for, but you still have to bear and witness the consequences in this life, how does this speak to you?*
> ❓ *If you are the victim of another's sin, how does this speak to you?*

There will be something, or someone, you need to pray about. Do so now.

Kings: the catastrophe

For 14 generations after David, Jesus' ancestors were kings. But—with a couple of exceptions—the best of them were compromisers, and the worst were catastrophic.

We are going to look at two of them who are fairly representative: Jotham and his son Ahaz. By this stage, David's kingdom had broken in two, with a king from David's line on the throne of the southern kingdom, Judah, with its capital in Jerusalem.

Compromise

Read 2 Kings 15:32-38

> ❓ *What was positive about Jotham's reign (v 34, end v 35)?*
> ❓ *What is the "but" in verse 35?*

The "high places" were shrines to the "gods" of the surrounding nations. God's people were syncretistic—worshipping the God of the Bible and hedging their bets by worshipping other gods too. Like people today, their did not reject God outright—they just worshipped other things alongside him.

And so Jotham's problem was not so much that he did not support worship of the true God but that he did not stop worship of other gods. He compromised—and while that may be a good thing in politics, it is always sinful in worship.

Catastrophe

Read 2 Kings 16:1-4

Ahaz worshipped at those pagan shrines his father had rejected but had not torn down (v 4). Here's an ancestor of Jesus, sacrificing his own son in worship of a false god (v 3).

Read 2 Kings 16:5-20

God's king trusted the king of Assyria rather than the King of the world (v 7-11), and reinvented Judah's worship to be patterned on Assyria's religion rather than the pattern God had given to Moses (v 12-18). God's people had become indistinguishable from the nations around them.

And so, five generations later, God caused his people to go and live in the nations around them—in the catastrophe of the exile. Why? **Read 2 Kings 24:20.**

And yet God was still at work. His plans cannot be undone by human sin. And yet people can be undone by sin. The lesson of Judah's kings is that complacency and compromise are deadly—and that their effects ripple through the generations. And perhaps that's something we need to hear in December, for how easy we find it to worship the Lord and also those modern gods of possessions, food, family, comfort and pleasure in the Christmas season.

Apply

> ❓ *How might you be in danger of falling into the God+something else worship trap?*
> ❓ *Are there areas you know you're compromising in when it comes to obeying God? Will you right that now, today, rather than thinking it can wait till January?*

Exile: there is a future

Many families contain in their known history a crisis moment, when it would have been very easy for the family line to end there and then.

For my family, it's the Second World War. What, humanly speaking, looked like blind chance meant my grandparents survived, when many others in their situation did not.

For Israel, that crisis moment was the exile, when Babylon invaded Judah, took Jerusalem, destroyed the temple and took many of the people (including Judah's royal family) to exile in Babylon. Even six centuries after the exile had ended, in Matthew's day, the nation had not recovered. You can see how it haunted Jewish culture by the way Matthew mentions "the exile" four times in the first 18 verses of his Gospel.

The great prophet of the exile of God's people was Ezekiel. God spends most of the first 30 chapters of Ezekiel explaining why Judah is in Babylon, though 2 Kings 24:20 sums it up pretty well!

And then come some rays of hope...

Read Ezekiel 37:1-10

- ❓ *What is the obvious answer to God's question in verse 3?*
- ❓ *But what is God's word powerful to do (v 4-6)?*

Read Ezekiel 37:11-14

- ❓ *What is this all an image of?*
- ❓ *What can Israel's people look forward to (v 12, 14)?*
- ❓ *What is the point of all this—both the exile and the return? (Spot the repeated phrase in v 6, 13, 14.)*

By the time of Jesus' birth, Israel had been back for centuries—and yet, in another sense, they'd not returned at all. The temple was a shadow of its former self, and the land had been occupied by various invading armies, most recently the Romans. And, of course, the people were still sinning.

So perhaps this is why Matthew mentions the exile four times. He wants to link Jesus' birth to the true end of exile—to God's people receiving true life and a real land of their own. And, perhaps, he wants to prepare his readers for the shape of Jesus' own experience—first the exile of crucifixion, and then the return of resurrection. Ezekiel prophesied about the nation—but you can also apply verses 4-10 to its Messiah. Jesus bore the ultimate exile so that he could bring God's people to the eternal promised land.

⌃ Pray

"Then you will know that I am the LORD." That was the purpose of God's judgment in the exile and God's mercy in the return. It was also the purpose of God's coming at the first Christmas. He wants us to know who he is. He wants us to worship him, and know him, and love and serve him. That's what we were made for. That's where we find life.

This Christmas, pray that amid the busyness you would get to know the Lord better by gazing at his Son.

Zerubabbel: the hope

Most Christmases, media articles outline the dwindling popularity or acceptability of Christianity, and Christian blogs bewail the secularisation of Christmas itself.

And it's tempting, in that kind of cultural climate, to give up a little, because how can we fight the tide? What difference can we make? You can't turn the clock back.

To that feeling, the prophet Haggai comes with a word of hope.

Read Haggai 2:20-23

This is (obviously!) at the end of Haggai, who is speaking to those who have returned to Judah after the exile.

> ❷ *To whom is this word of the Lord addressed (v 21)?*
> ❷ *What is God going to do?*
> • *v 21*   • *v 22*   • *v 23*

Haggai was speaking into a "day of small things" (Zechariah 4:10), when the people of God were all too aware that things just weren't how they used to be. When the temple was being rebuilt, those returning exiles old enough to remember the previous temple had wept, for it was such a poor replacement (Ezra 3:12). But... there was hope, because there was Zerubbabel. He was the governor selected by the Persian overlords of the Jews, but more crucially he was in the line of David— and God had chosen him to be his signet ring: the ring used to give seals of approval in wax on letters and orders. Things would not remain as they were (Haggai 2:22). Better days lay behind them, yet *far* better days lay ahead of them.

The exile did not signal the end of God's plans to bring his Messiah to the world.

Zerubbabel (whose name means "born in Babylon") was back in Jerusalem, and God's great salvation was another generation nearer to coming to fruition.

Read Haggai 1:13-15

> ❷ *What impact did Haggai's prophecy have on the people under Zerubbabel's leadership (v 14-15)?*

God, through his prophet, was pointing forwards to the ultimate greater son of David— not Zerubbabel, but Jesus. Make no mistake: Christmas was a moment that shook, and shakes, the heavens and the earth. It is the declaration that there is a God who gets involved in this world. There is a King who rules this earth. Through the life and death of the One who lay in that manger, we can know for sure that one day every knee will bow to Zerubbabel's descendant Jesus.

Read 1 Corinthians 15:58

> ❷ *Because we know that Jesus wins, what should we do?*

We do not have a temple to build, as in Haggai's day. But we do have a church to build, until the day God's Messiah comes again, to shake the heavens and the earth. You can, stirred and equipped by God's Spirit, make an eternal difference today as you serve and share the Lord Jesus.

⌄ Apply

> ❷ *How will you "give yourself fully to the work of the Lord" today?*

Bible in a year: Micah 1-3 • Luke 21 v 20-38

Mary: the Lord's servant

HAPPY CHRISTMAS! We're jumping forwards to the final generation in Jesus' family tree: "Mary was the mother of Jesus who is called the Messiah" (Matthew 1:16).

Favoured by God
Read Luke 1:26-37

> ❓ *Which aspects of God's promises to David does Gabriel pick up on as he announces the coming Messiah to that Messiah's mother (v 32-33)?*

The angel states that "no word from God will ever fail" (v 37).

> ❓ *How does the history of Jesus' family demonstrate the truth of this claim?*

Read Luke 1:38

> ❓ *How does Mary's response display the same faith as was shown centuries before by Abraham (Genesis 12:4)?*

Christmas was not easy for Mary. She almost lost her marriage (Matthew 1:19). She certainly lost control. And she would very soon learn that, sometime and somehow, she would feel as though her own soul had been pierced (Luke 2:34-35). Each Easter, I wonder whether Mary remembered that prophecy as she stood and watched her son die the most agonising death.

Mary must have known some of the cost as well as the privilege of what she was being asked to do. But she responded with obedience. Christmas calls us to do the same in response to the announcement that the Messiah has been born. I am the Lord's servant. Christmas is not really about comfort. It's about serving. The Messiah has come, and that means that the most glorious, fulfilling life you can lead is one of knowing and loving and serving him.

Rejoicing in God
Read Luke 1:46-55

Mary celebrates the One who is growing inside her and the God whose Son he is. And in her song, she picks up on various responses that we've seen in those who were called to be part of God's purposes, in his Son's family line:

> ❓ *In her song, where can you spot...*
> • *amazement?*
> • *humility?*
> • *joy?*
> • *praise?*

These are the responses we, too, should sing out today, as we celebrate the great truth that, on that day in history, "the time came for the baby to be born and [Mary gave birth to her firstborn, a son. She wrapped him in cloths and placed him in a manger" (Luke 2:6-7). Here at last is the cradle into which we can look and say, *This is the Messiah, the son of David, the son of Abraham.* HAPPY CHRISTMAS!

⌃ Pray

Take Mary's song as the inspiration for your praise of the God the Father and God the Son today.

Wide as well as back

We've walked through Jesus' family, back and back to Abraham. But of course family trees don't only work back; they work outwards too. Which is where we come in.

His family

Read Hebrews 2:9-13

Here is a wonderful description of what happened at the first Christmas: "Jesus ... was made lower than the angels for a little while" (v 9). We cannot comprehend the heights he left, the distance he travelled from heavenly throne to stable manger—or the humility and the love that caused him to do so.

And here is a wonderful description of the other end of Jesus' earthly life, his ascension: "Jesus [is] now crowned with glory and honour because he suffered death ... for everyone" (v 9).

And here is a wonderful description of our relationship to God the Father and to Jesus.

> ❷ *What is it?*
> • *v 10*
> • *v 11*

So we have been brought into Abraham's family tree. By faith, we are Jesus' siblings. And what a big brother he is—the one perfect pioneer of our salvation (v 10).

His humanity

Read Hebrews 2:14-17

> ❷ *Why did Jesus need to be born a human at the first Christmas (v 14)?*
> ❷ *What did his perfect obedience and sin-bearing death achieve (v 15)?*

And so...

Read Hebrews 2:1; 3:1; 4:14

> ❷ *What does the writer to the Hebrews urge us to do this Christmas?*
> ❷ *How do the truths of 2:9-17 motivate you to do this?*

The genealogy of Jesus

Read through the family line of Jesus in Matthew 1:1-17, slowly.

> ❷ *What have you learned about...*
> • *how God works?*
> • *who God works through?*
> • *what is the right response to being brought into his family and purposes?*

⌄ Apply

> ❷ *Which character that we've looked at most resonates with you right now? Why?*
> ❷ *How might the Spirit be working to help you, or shape you, or change you, through meditating on what God did for and through that particular person?*

⌃ Pray

Spend time praising God for the coming of Jesus, the Messiah. Recommit to holding firmly to the faith you profess. Ask God to use you, his child, to serve your big brother, the Lord Jesus, as you enjoy each day all the ways he has served and is serving you.

1 CORINTHIANS: Marriage

What's your attitude towards marriage and singleness? In what ways is it the same as that of your surrounding culture? In what ways is it different?

Western society is very muddled about marriage. It's still seen as the fairy-tale ideal and yet is not expected to be a lifelong commitment. In this chapter, we learn what God thinks about marriage, singleness and divorce. First of all, marriage.

Sex is good

Read 1 Corinthians 7:1-6

❓ *What problem is Paul addressing (v 1)?*

In chapter 6, we saw the idea that only the soul mattered—so it didn't matter if you slept around. Here, the same idea has led to the opposite extreme—asceticism, where bodily pleasures are to be avoided because they contaminate the soul. So some thought that married couples should be celibate.

❓ *How well has the church been doing at abstinence (7:2; see also 5:1; 6:15-16)?*
❓ *So what's the solution (7:2-5)?*
❓ *Do you find verses 3-4 controversial? In what way?*

It's right, good and even obligatory for married couples to enjoy God's gift of sex. And, in contrast to the world, it's not about how you feel but how you can lovingly serve. The key to success is both partners putting their spouse before themselves.

☑ Apply

❓ *Christians are often viewed as prudish and God as "anti-sex". How do these*

verses speak to that view?
❓ *If you're married, how does this section encourage and/or challenge you?*

Singleness is better

There'll be more on singleness towards the end of chapter 7, but here are the headlines.

Read 1 Corinthians 7:7-9

❓ *Paul himself is single. So what is he saying in verse 7a?*
❓ *How does verse 8 reiterate this?*
❓ *What are the "gifts" Paul is talking about in verse 7?*

We hear lots about singleness being an "unwanted gift". But it's not unwanted by Paul. Both singleness and marriage are states of being graciously given to us by God, to be used in his way. What is key is that married people shouldn't act as though they have the gift of singleness by being celibate, and single people shouldn't act as though they have the gift of marriage by having sex.

❓ *But what if you're "burning with passion" and have no opportunity to get married (v 9)?*

More on this later in the chapter!

▲ Pray

Ask God to use this time in 1 Corinthians 7 to give you contentment about your marital status.

God's view of divorce

Divorce is an accepted part of modern life and affects us all in one way or another. So this passage is radical.

The ideal
Read 1 Corinthians 7:10-11

❷ *What is the overriding principle?*
❷ *Read Matthew 19:3-6. How do Paul's words here match what Jesus said in Matthew 19?*

For Christians, divorce is just not an option. Both Paul and Jesus go on to qualify this position, because they know that life in a fallen world is broken and messy (see Matthew 19:7-9 and later in 1 Corinthians 7); but marriage is meant to be a lasting covenant.

The broken reality
Read 1 Corinthians 7:12-16

When Paul says, "I, not the Lord", he simply means that Jesus didn't talk about this issue specifically during his time on earth (see also v 25). Paul is God's Spirit-inspired apostle, so his words are authoritative.

❷ *What situation is Paul talking about in verses 12-13?*

Many of the Corinthians had come to faith when they were already married and so didn't have the option of choosing a believing husband or wife. They were worried that their spouse was making them "unclean" (a Jewish idea), and so they resorted to divorce. But Paul says that the Christian has a "cleansing" effect on the rest of the family. This doesn't make the unbelieving spouse

a Christian, but it enables the Christian spouse to remain married.

❷ *What is the concession in verse 15?*

It's heartbreaking, but if the unbelieving spouse wants to separate, then the Christian is to let them go, rather than create strife. They might never become a Christian anyway (v 16), and forcing them to stay in a marriage they don't want probably won't be the best way of helping them.

❷ *What do you think is meant by the phrase "not bound" (v 15)?*

Some Christians take this to mean that under certain circumstances (e.g. abandonment or adultery, see Matthew 19:9), the Christian is free to marry again: some, that this simply means the marriage can be ended. What is clear is that divorce should only be a last resort, when all attempts at reconciliation have failed.

▾ Apply

We need to support and protect marriages but also remember that divorce isn't an unforgivable sin. There is abundant grace at the foot of the cross.

❷ *What common reasons for divorce does this text say God would not agree with?*
❷ *Divorce is a personally painful subject for many of us. Do you need to ask a trusted and mature Christian friend to talk or pray with you about something?*

Bible in a year: Zechariah 5-8 • Luke 23 v 1-25 ✔

A friend in need

Friendship is a theme of a number of these proverbs; so, as you read the passage, note down the things it says about what true friends are like, and how to be a true friend.

Read Proverbs 18:22 – 19:10

Mates?

❓ *Think about your friendships as you reflect on some of the lessons in this passage.*

Quality not quantity (18:24). No doubt you have many acquaintances and people you know—but sometimes running round to maintain a wide circle of friends can rob you of the pleasure and support that just one or two close friendships can give.

Based on what? (19:4). Some people draw close for what they can get out of you—and not just money. We can suck out a friend's time and energy, and have no concern for their needs.

How do you gain friends? (19:6). We can try to win favour with gifts—of compliments or entertainment—or use a position of power or authority to win people into our "inner circle". But such things are never genuine friendship.

The test of need (19:7). Where friendship is genuine, it will rise above such things as disaster, social disgrace and even personal hurts and wrongs. In a word, friends are loyal.

···· TIME OUT ····································

See Jesus' example of these points in **Luke 15:11-16**.

Best friends

There is something wholesome, fulfilling and nurturing about true friendship, so that in a relationship of trust, we may truly say with Solomon that "wounds from a friend can be trusted" (Proverbs 27:6).

✓ Apply

❓ *So how do your friends, and your own friendship, match up to these criteria?*
❓ *Do you have something to pray about or something to talk about with someone as a result of reading these verses?*

⌃ Pray

Read John 15:9-17 and make it the basis of your prayers.

Thank God that he is pleased to call you a friend through Jesus.

Thank God for your close friends and friendships.

Pray that you would be a good friend to those who need one, and that the Lord would fill you with his power to love others.

Ask God to lead you to people who need your friendship.

Contented?

Here, we zoom out for a heart check-up. How much of your identity comes from your external circumstances? And how does that affect how content you feel in life?

Picture 1: Circumcision

Read 1 Corinthians 7:17-20

- ❷ *What point is Paul making using the metaphor of circumcision (v 18-19)?*
- ❷ *What general principle does Paul draw from this (v 17, 20)?*

Jewish circumcision used to be a sign that you were part of God's people. But now that Jesus has come, circumcision is irrelevant. It's simply an external circumstance which has no impact on spiritual health. What does matter is that we live "as a believer" in whatever circumstances God has given us (v 17), evidenced by our obedience to God (v 19b).

- ❷ *How might this apply to marital status?*

Remember that some of the Corinthians thought that changing their circumstances would make them more spiritual, e.g. refraining from sex within marriage or even getting divorced. But this reveals that they were idolising their circumstances, and putting all their energy into changing their situation in life instead of focusing on living for God in the circumstances he'd given them.

Picture 2: Slavery

Read 1 Corinthians 7:21-24

- ❷ *How does the metaphor of slavery drive home Paul's point about our identity not being in our circumstances (v 21-22)?*

Paul isn't saying that slavery doesn't matter—indeed, he encourages slaves to gain their freedom if possible (v 21) and not to willingly enter into slavery (v 23). But again, these are external circumstances, which do not impinge on their core identity—which is freedom to be slaves of Christ.

- ❷ *How would this apply to a single Christian who really wants to get married? Does Paul mean that if you're single when you become a Christian, you should stay single (v 24—see v 9, 28)?*

So then, why is this passage here, in the middle of a chapter on marriage and singleness? Again, it's all about identity. As we see from the slavery example, it's not wrong to change your circumstances—just don't do it because you think it'll change your spiritual identity or it's the secret to contentment, because it won't and it isn't. This needs to speak to all of us. As someone who wrestled discontentedly with singleness for many years, I can see how my identity was so bound up with my marital status that I lost the contentment I could have been enjoying in Christ alone.

⌄ Apply

- ❷ *How deeply is your sense of identity and wellbeing bound up with your circumstances? What would change if you increasingly sought contentment in knowing and serving Christ?*

Bible in a year: Zechariah 13-14 • Luke 24 v 1-35

God on singleness

Now Paul looks in more detail at what he began to explain in verses 8-9: why and how can he say that singleness is better than marriage?

Time is short
Read 1 Corinthians 7:25-31

- ❓ *What do you think the "present crisis" might be (v 26)?*
- ❓ *What effect does this have on the choice to marry (v 27-28)?*
- ❓ *How does this relate back to the passage we looked at in the previous study?*

This crisis could be something specifically Corinthian, e.g. a famine—but it's more likely to mean the time we live in now, between Jesus' ascension and his sudden return: a time of persecution and sacrifice, when marriage will cause certain difficulties.

- ❓ *What point is Paul making in verses 29-31?*

Paul is using rhetorical language to say, in effect, *Don't live as though this world is all there is, because it's not going to last!* Of course husbands are to love their wives (Ephesians 5:25), but those who are married need to remember that marriage is temporary, and their relationship with Jesus is the only eternal thing they have.

🔼 Pray

- ❓ *How does the reality of Jesus' impending return affect you day to day?*

Pray for a greater awareness that you live on the edge of eternity.

Marriage takes up time!
Read 1 Corinthians 7:32-40

- ❓ *How does marriage affect the way someone spends their time (v 32-35)?*

Married people have a duty, and hopefully a desire, to focus their time and energy on loving their spouse and any children—this is what God calls them to do. A single person, on the other hand, has much more time and energy to devote to evangelism, discipling younger Christians, and serving the church and the world. Paul is saying that single people considering marriage should be aware of this.

- ❓ *How does Paul re-emphasise the "rightness" of marriage while affirming the benefits of singleness (v 36-38)?*
- ❓ *What important condition does he give widows (and, by implication, any single people) who wish to get married (v 39)?*

In summary: it's fine to get married to a fellow believer if it'll help you to obey and serve God, but you'll do even better to stay single, because eternity beckons.

☑ Apply

- ❓ *If you're single, does this passage need to reshape your view of yourself, your time, and your dreams in any way? How?*
- ❓ *If you're married, what will you do to make sure single people in your church feel included and encouraged?*

Introduce a friend to

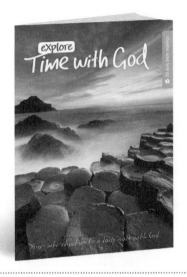

explore

If you're enjoying using *Explore*, why not introduce a friend? *Time with God* is our introduction to daily Bible reading and is a great way to get started with a regular time with God. It includes 28 daily readings along with articles, advice and practical tips on how to apply what the passage teaches.

Why not order a copy for someone you would like to encourage?

Coming up next...

- Lamentations
  with Robin Ham

- Hosea and Haggai
  with Dave Griffith-Jones

- Amos
  with Carl Laferton and Rachel Jones

- 1 Corinthians
  with Paul Jump and Anna Marsh

- Proverbs
  with Tim Thornborough

- New Year
  with Carl Laferton

 Don't miss your copy. Contact your local Christian bookshop or church agent, or visit:

UK & Europe: thegoodbook.co.uk
info@thegoodbook.co.uk
Tel: 0333 123 0880

North America: thegoodbook.com
info@thegoodbook.com
Tel: 866 244 2165

Australia: thegoodbook.com.au
info@thegoodbook.com.au
Tel: (02) 9564 3555

New Zealand: thegoodbook.co.nz
info@thegoodbook.co.nz
Tel: +61 2 9564 3555

Join the *explore* community

The *Explore* Facebook group is a community of people who use *Explore* to study the Bible each day.

This is the place to share your thoughts, questions, encouragements and prayers as you read *Explore*, and interact with other readers, as well as contributors, from around the world. No questions are too simple or too difficult to ask.

JOIN NOW:
www.facebook.com/groups/tgbc.explore